CONNECTING AND INFLUENCING

A Leader's Guide to Genuine Communication

Katrin Winkler & Nicola Bramwell

Linchpin Books

Illustrations by Olywebart Design
Cover image courtesy of PantherMedia
Book layout and cover by Olywebart Design

ISBN 978-94-6407-542-7
D/2021/15004/01

© The Bayard Holding bv – publishing house Linchpin Books, 2021
All rights reserved. No part of this publication may be reproduced, stored in a retrieval system, or transmitted in any form or by any means, electronic, mechanical, photocopying, recording, scanning or otherwise, except as permitted by law, without either the prior written permission of the author and the publisher.

Linchpin Books is a trade name of The Bayard Holding bv. Registered in Belgium,
No. BE 0629 734 985

www.linchpinbooks.eu

EXPERT VIEWS ON CONNECTING AND INFLUENCING

"This might not be the bible to communication, but it comes pretty close.
The sobering fact is 'words change worlds' – so how are your words impacting others? If you genuinely care about how to positively influence and impact others, this book provides an invaluable toolkit of ideas and insights that you'll keep coming back to".
Professor Paul McGee, aka The Sumo Guy, Sunday Times best-selling author, coach and international speaker.

"The French mathematician Blaise Pascal (1623-1662) wrote in a letter: « Je n'ai fait celle-ci plus longue que parce que je n'ai pas eu le loisir de la faire plus courte ». (I have made this longer than usual because I have not had time to make it shorter).
Effective, meaningful and impactful communication is both art and science. As any art, it is used to express technical proficiency, beauty, emotional power, or conceptual ideas in many different forms. As any science, there are rules which can be learnt, understood and applied. This book is a practical 'art and science guide' for leaders to master communication so that people understand information and can act accordingly with passion and purpose".
Dr Thomas Dobmeyer, CEO Pharmalex Group

"A must read for anybody looking for insights on how to become a highly effective communicator. In an increasingly global and virtual world, we need to adapt how we communicate for more fruitful collaboration and exchange. And in our hectic daily lives, one of the greatest gifts we can give to someone else is our undivided and undistracted attention, to listen intently to understand, not just to reply. This book gives the background and the tools to build the skills for making communications even more impactful."
Line Stigen Raquet, CEO Creoptix AG

AUTHORS

Dr. Katrin Winkler

Professor Dr. Katrin Winkler is a Human Resources and Leadership professor at the University of Applied Sciences (UAS) Kempten, Germany. As both academic professor and having many years' experience leading international teams and consulting for leaders around the world, she shares her insights on effective communication and how to motivate and inspire people.

Nicola Bramwell

Nicola Bramwell has an MBA and business background in strategic marketing, general management and leadership. She has held senior positions in blue chip companies in complex industries and shares much expertise in leading change and developing effective communication skills for personal impact. Nicola is also an accredited DISC & EQ Behavioural Analyst and workshop facilitator.

TABLE OF CONTENTS

Introduction	**Why Care?**	**6**

Part 1: The Real-Life Work Situations (and Models to Help) — **11**

Chapter 1	A bad day at the office?	12
Chapter 2	It's easy with one person, right?	20
Chapter 3	It's how you treat others	30
Chapter 4	The trouble with groups	50
Chapter 5	Let's put it in writing	72

Part 2: The Overarching Principle of Communication (the Deep Dive) — **91**

Chapter 6	What you need to know	92
Chapter 7	Developing your skills	112
Chapter 8	Your mindset counts	130
Chapter 9	Presence or being present?	142
Chapter 10	More new world challenges	152

A Final Note — 160

Bibliography and Notes — **162**

Acknowledgements — 174

Index of Key Terms — 176

Introduction

WHY CARE?

Why does communication matter? Well, simply put, if you are a leader, you need to know that leadership is communication! And as a leader, what you say, what you don't say, and how you behave towards others is all sending a message. If you don't make an effort, or your communication is poor, it has incredible effects on how others perceive you and your abilities. Rightly or wrongly, communication skills, followed by appearance are the qualities most often associated with professionalism (1). You need to care!

Communication is as natural as breathing. It is part of what makes us human. Great communication can excite, inspire and help us fall in love. Poor communication can make us feel unimportant (2), worse still, useless, excluded, worthless or unloved. However, in the business world, though we know communication is important, even essential, we often fall into old habits or just quick responses. Only when we meet challenges and conflicts do we stop and think about new ways of behaving or consider how to change and communicate better.

> *The price of doing the same old thing is far higher than the price of change.*
>
> William J. Clinton (3)

The reality is that no one is born with the skills to deal with all the people we encounter (2). We need to learn how to communicate well in an iterative and life-long approach. The good news is that we can learn how to **connect** with others better when we care to do so. All too often this will start with a negative experience when we get it wrong! Key is reflecting on what we did wrong, taking time to consider how we could improve, investing in our own development to gain new skills, having new tools and models to utilize, and actually trying them out! What is interesting to note, is that all these steps in our learning process start with us. Great communication really does **start with the individual** and can be applied equally well by individual managers, project leaders or senior executives with the desire to connect better with others. It is about **choosing to care** about how you communicate – not how important you appear, but how you positively influence others and make others feel. It's all about the goal and the meaning you convey when you set out to share information, seek input, discuss ideas, build relationships, show appreciation or open up about hopes and dreams. It is about what you say, how you say it, what you leave out, even the format you use. So, great communication is a combination of your **mindset, skills and presence** to maximize the right approach for varying work-related scenarios.

Added complexity comes from the receivers of any communication too. People "hear" from their perspective (4) and this is affected by the **relationship between sender and receiver**, as well as the perceived quality of the factual information being relayed. Education, culture, personality and mood all affect communication effectiveness. The rise of virtual scenarios caused by globalization, digitalization and even pandemics, also increase the challenges when it comes to communicating well.

Does this all matter? Yes. Many studies highlight that workplace productivity and morale are highly impacted by the communication from **senior leaders**. Employee engagement is higher when leaders are seen to behave well (5). Leaders listening and communicating clearly impacts organizational commitment and when communication fails, mistrust sets in (6). Other studies have shown that the degree to which employees embrace organizational change is largely dependent on their trust in leaders (7) and organizational change is more successfully implemented when leaders act as role models and continue to communicate frequently (8). Trust is fundamental and can only be fostered through great communication, achieving positive influence on others and creating a safe environment where others are willing to speak up and open up.

Figure 1. Trust is the precursor to engagement and organizational commitment

So where does caring come into all of this? Well, it's two-fold. Firstly, it is caring about how you behave. Your communication style is your behaviour towards other people, the **first impression** you give for instance. It is conscious and linked to how you motivate and influence others. How you choose to relate to others is key to human development, even staying sane (9). Positive relationships build a nurturing environment (9) and a World Economic Forum study in 2019 concluded that "relationships have the biggest effect on health" (10). Secondly, it is caring about how other people feel and how you make them feel. It starts with empathy, a key aspect of **emotional intelligence** and one, guru Daniel Goleman claims represents the foundation skill of all social competencies. Emotional intelligence in the workplace, is "twice as important for excellent performance as technical skills and conventional IQ" (11). In this context, empathy is resonating with someone else, their pain for example, yet you don't have to like the person (12). To show care however, you need to go to the next level, to cultivate an attitude of loving kindness, or **compassion**, towards people. In this context, compassion incorporates the intention to act (12). It means communicating with the intention to connect with someone, to understand a person or situation, to make the situation better. It is being generous and often humble; it requires time and a conscious shift from reactive responses to well thought through messages and conversations.

This may sound difficult. It may sound way beyond the confines of daily and workplace communication. In this book we will share key elements for both your personal consideration and for practicing better communication with others. By reflecting on real-life scenarios, you can begin to translate tools to your own workplace and to challenges you may encounter day to day. As you progress through the chapters of this book you will learn about why trust is fundamental for communication, how your own mindset, skills and presence shapes your communication style and how to choose an appropriate style for both situational and individual differences.

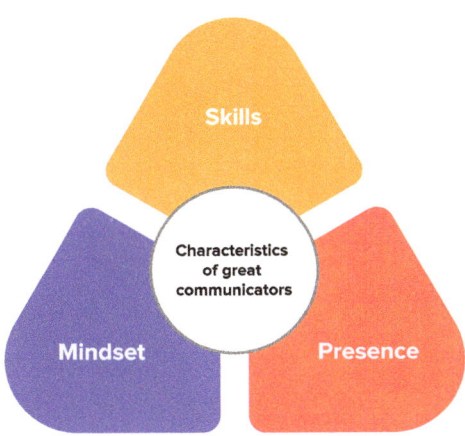

Figure 2: Characteristics of great communicators

From a practical perspective, we will consider how to develop skills and apply effective models for three levels of communication; relationship building in one-to-one scenarios, collaborating in teams and group settings, and how to achieve reach across the broader organization or externally with written formats and mass media. We also explore the mix of real-time (synchronous) and delayed (asynchronous) communications required.

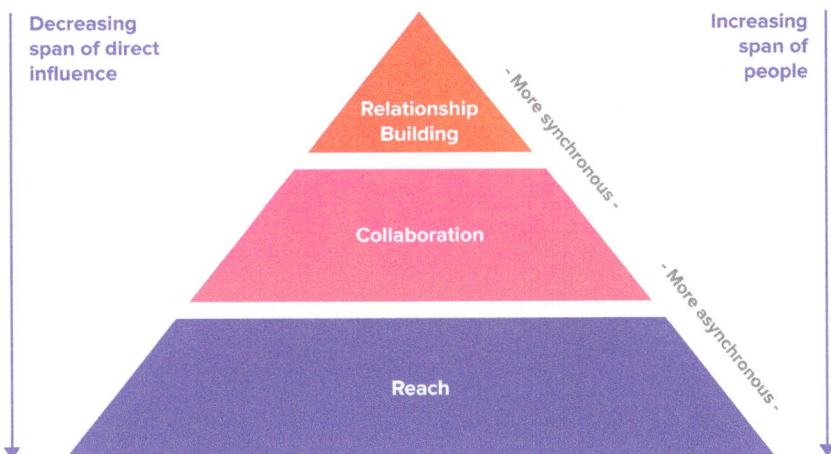

Figure 3: Ability to connect and maintain influence at all levels is required in business

Finally, we will do a deeper dive into the principle of communication, understanding communication as the most important transferable ability for success in all business settings. This will ensure you have access to key knowledge that can help explain why communication goes wrong so often and how you can develop to be a great communicator when you choose to care. With knowledge and skills, a positive mindset and significant presence you will be better positioned to connect with other people, build relationships, collaborate and reach wider audiences.

PART 1

The Real-Life Work Situations (and Models to Help)

Welcome to part one of this compendium to genuine communication. Communication is all about conveying meaning, about sharing information and affecting outcomes. How and what we communicate impacts our relationships, both personal and business, creates impressions, good or bad, and impacts our ability to positively influence others. Though we constantly communicate through our words, body language, written messages and images, effective communication is a learned skill that requires knowledge, application and continuous development. The good news is it can be learnt! As author Paul McGee explains, "no one is born with all the skills to deal with the challenges of life and the people we encounter, yet we can all keep learning to do better" (2).

Chapter 1

A BAD DAY AT THE OFFICE?

Key knowledge

- Communicating is more than just informing, talking about work tasks, or telling people what to do
- Communication is a meaningful exchange between people, to connect and build lasting relationships
- Communication easily goes wrong when the understanding, goals or process is missing

 Key models

- 5 axioms of why communication goes wrong
- Situational influence model for leaders one-to-one, in groups and for extended reach

 Impact

- Being aware of when communication could be better is the starting point for learning

To stimulate the learning process, we will review real-life work situations. It is essential for the learning process to reflect on why communication can go wrong and analyze your role in it. This continuous reflection helps to create awareness of triggers or situations that limit your effectiveness and you gain a better understanding on how you are perceived by others. Only when you can identify the problem can you begin to affect a change.

Let's start by looking at examples.

Stefan (not his real name) came to a communication workshop because he was told he was a poor presenter. His own assessment was that his audience had a short attention span and lacked the brainpower to keep up with him. Review of his style showed highly technical presentations, no use of imagery and always running over time.

The issue?

Skill — Though technically correct, what Stefan presented was not inspiring, it was not always relevant for his audience and he relied too much on verbal communication which was difficult to follow. Stefan did not have great communication skills to craft a memorable and simple message that others could buy in to.

How to do better:

Formal presentations can be a challenge as you may not know the audience well, however it is always better to:

- Keep is short and simple (KISS)
- Start with a "why" message — why the audience should listen / what's in it for them
- Go beyond facts and connect emotionally, such as give meaningful examples
- Mix verbal messages with bullet points, pictures and graphs
- Never run over time!

What this example highlights is that great communication requires **planning and preparation** and the needs of the audience must always come first. A monologue is boring, and most people will switch off very quickly. Great communicators learn how to adapt their message and their behaviour to best suit individual or situational differences. It is not about being unauthentic, it is learning how best to communicate so others want to listen and pay attention.

Maria (again not her real name) was stuggling to express her opinions in project meetings. Her belief was that she was avoiding conflict by not speaking up. However, it was causing her to become personally frustrated and unhappy.

The issue?

Mindset – The block is Maria's unwillingness to address issues and differences, which is not the same thing as conflict. Instead, she is making assumptions on how other people think and act. Without asking questions to understand a situation, it is impossible to look at the issues from another perspectives.

How to do better:

Seeking to understand a situation or another person's perspective can acknowledge differences, avoid conflict and reduce personal frustrations:

- Seek clarity by asking questions and listening empathetically
- Address personal perspectives objectively
- Be open to inputs and ideas from others
- Focus on common ground, shared goals and results

Your mindset is your collection of thoughts and beliefs that shape your habits and have great influence on your actions. A key aspect of mindset includes assumptions or notions arising out of experiences, culture or philosophy of life. The **assumption of "my way" is best is never true**. When individuals think about problems or reaching goals, patterns are formed. These patterns are self-imposed boundaries or barriers, that keep our thinking in a framework and our behaviour, such as our communication style, is constrained in this way and not adapted to individuals or situations (13).

In an assessment centre there was a participant who was constantly lounging in his chair and only now and then would throw a statement into the group conversation. As observers, we noted this odd behaviour and considered it's meaning:

1) He did not want to participate...
2) He believed the group was beneath him...
3) He was unaware of how he came across...

Afterwards, in a feedback session we addressed the fact that he came across as arrogant and unwilling to participate in the group discussions. He was utterly surprised. It was his blind spot!

The issue?

Presence — At work we need to appear to be present and show a positive demeanour. This means active participation and demonstrating appropriate body language. It is all too easy to appear disengaged by how we sit and how willing or not we are to get involved.

How to do better:

Presence is physical and participation is an active mechanism for expressing opinions and exerting influence:

- Positive body language signals include real smiles, eye contact, leaning in or forward, active noises (uh, ya...) and active conversation
- Avoid negative signals such as broken eye contact, turning away, checking your watch or sighing, arms crossed, leaning back or a blank / cold face
- Engage with others: ask questions, facilitate discussions, seek to gain insights from all group members, share personal inputs / expertise, summarize key points

Human communication involves verbal and non-verbal elements and to understand a message, both have to be considered. Sometimes when the verbal / non-verbal don't match, this confuses receivers and makes it difficult to understand the message or create misunderstandings. Non-verbal communication is also much stronger, more intuitive and more difficult to manipulate and includes body language, posture, gestures and eye contact.

PATTERNS AS TO WHY COMMUNICATION GOES WRONG?

There are **five axioms of communication**, or reasons, to explain how communication works and also how misunderstandings may come about and it's easy to see how they can arise in the workplace (14). Key is understanding that communication is based on meaning and interaction so must be framed in a social and cultural context.

Reason 1: Even silence is communication because **every behaviour is a form of communication**. It is impossible not to communicate. Even if communication is being avoided, such as silence, the silence itself and facial expressions can be analyzed by the receiver. For instance, in challenging times, if a leader does not communicate with the team, even just to reassure, that is seen as a negative message in itself.

Reason 2: Content is what we say, yet our **relationship with the message sender determines how we understand meaning**. Apart from the plain meaning of words, more information is delivered. A simple example to demonstrate. Imagine a manager tells someone: "I'd like to discuss your area of responsibility, maybe we can shift a few things around". If the individual does not trust that manager, they will probably react in a negative way, afraid they've done something wrong, suspecting that the manager is trying to punish them. On the other hand, if they trust the manager, they will be more open to discuss options as they are expecting positive actions from the manager.

Reason 3: We often **interpret or justify our reactions** to what is said by the sender's use of punctuation and structure to alter meaning. Punctuation is the process of organizing groups of messages into meanings, as we do when using punctuation in written language. However, the punctuation can sometimes alter the meaning considerably, such as the example of a panda who "eats shoots and leaves" or "eats, shoots and leaves". Senders and receivers often structure the communication flow differently and both interpret their own behaviour during the communication as merely a reaction to the other's behaviour. This can be very dangerous in conflicts – if both parties focus on what the other said in order to use it as an explanation for their reaction and justifying that they couldn't react in a different way, it causes a vicious cycle.

Reason 4: Human communication involves **verbal and non-verbal elements** and mismatches confuse us because non-verbal communication is stronger and more difficult to manipulate. Research has shown that our receptiveness to others, based on their words, is only 7%. Tone of voice is 38% and body language is 55%, including posture, gestures and eye contact (15). This is an obvious concern when communication goes digital!

Reason 5: Communication often works better between equals, as **power can lead to conflict**. If people are on different levels and attempt to gain control of an exchange by dominating the overall communication, conflict can arise. Avoiding hierarchic, top-down power is therefore essential. On the opposite side, it is also critical that employees have willingness and abilities to speak up, share opinions and question senior management.

Good communication is essential for satisfying human relationships and interactions. Great communication is about appealing to the heart, not just the head. These basic aspects aid understanding of why sometimes people do not understand each other and why issues arise every day. The fundamental issue when things go wrong is often "I didn't feel important" (2), limiting willingness to speak up or hindered by lack of listening by the other party. This challenge is also exaggerated in the virtual or digital world as loss of face-to-face feel and non-verbal clues makes it more difficult to make people feel comfortable or show someone else that they are important. Key is remembering that "virtual doesn't have to mean impersonal" to quote Simon Sinek (16).

Good communication is just as stimulating as black coffee, and just as hard to sleep after.

Anne Morrow Lindbergh (17)

HOW WE CAN CREATE BETTER IMPACT BY CONSIDERING DIFFERENT SETTINGS

When we consider how to overcome the challenges of communication errors in organizations, it is important to understand different levels of communication and the significance of planning and implementing accordingly. From an internal communication perspective, well developed and effective communication requires the use of different skills and tools to deliver consistent, impactful and inspiring messages in **different scenarios**. For example, as a leader:

- In one-to-one situations focus is placed to engage the other party
- In group meetings, skills here include actively leading discussions and facilitating outcomes to integrate all members to meet shared goals
- To reach a wider organizational setting, written formats become paramount and the use of technology more evident to inform or influence more broadly

Why must we be aware of these differences? It is because we need to be clear on what we are trying to achieve and how to go about making it work. Communication goals go beyond informing, sharing, discussing, requesting etc. Communication builds relationships and it is also the cornerstone of how we influence others! So, before we consider influence one-to-one, within teams and across organizations, it is important to understand the concept of **influence** itself.

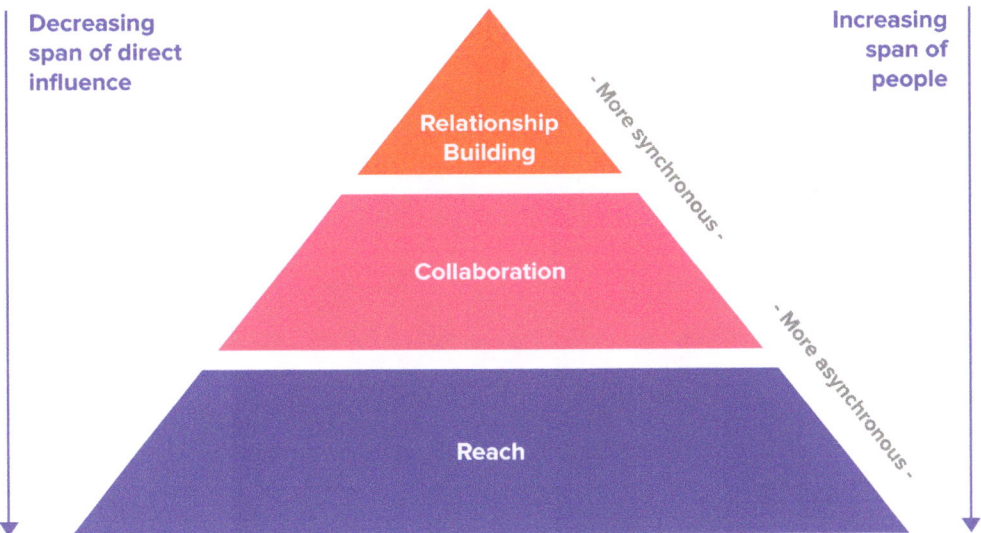

Figure 4: Situational influence model

We all have the ability to influence others. Whether it's in the workplace or at home, our actions influence other people's perception, feelings and thoughts. Because of this, we need to be careful in what we say and do. Leaders especially need to be more mindful and pay attention to themselves as they can make other people feel better or worse.

Influence is the power to cause someone to change a behaviour, belief, or opinion, based on motivation and common vision (18). Just to be clear, this is not the same as persuasion (19), which can be used to spur someone to action but without actually earning their sincere buy-in. Behaviours that are impacted by positive influence include decision making and problem-solving, enabling more collaborative and creative approaches. This is critical for more flexible project work for instance, due to more reliance on informal leadership approaches, because influence is not linked to hierarchy. The challenge however comes when we consider the effects of larger organizations, distance management and remote workers, where direct influence reduces. To understand the goals, skills, mindset, tools, mix of real-time and non-immediate exchange, as well as pitfalls, we will look at each level in subsequent chapters. For one-to-ones, see chapter 3, groups see chapter 4 and wider reach is covered in chapter 5.

> *You don't have to be a 'person of influence' to be influential. In fact, the most influential people in my life are probably not even aware of the things they've taught me.*
>
> Scott Adams (20)

Chapter 2

IT'S EASY WITH ONE PERSON, RIGHT?

Key knowledge

- To connect with people and build lasting relationships, the goal of conversation must be genuine dialogue
- Genuine dialogue only occurs through empathy and when the intention is to understand the other person or the situation
- Asking questions and listening is the most important skill for leaders to avoid judgements or incorrect assumptions, especially when having difficult conversations

 Key models

- Genuine dialogue
- Emotional intelligence
- Empathetic listening

 Impact

- Engaging others makes people feel important and listened to. It is part of establishing trust

If communication is all about exchanging information, connecting with someone else and building a relationship, surely it is easier with one person? Yes, yet only when based on intent to connect with the other person. It starts from you and it takes work. As we have already touched on, all too easily it can go wrong without self-awareness, skills or clear goals.

> *A dialogue leads to connection, which leads to trust, which leads to engagement.*
>
> Seth Godin (21)

It needs to start with creating **dialogue**, a conversation between two people. The challenge is how to make it feel right, so people open up, speak up about themselves, their needs, their concerns etc. It is also thinking how to overcome hidden reactions and not missing non-verbal clues, and in the virtual world it includes lever- aging the appropriate digital technology for a face-to-face feel. As Brazilian educator and philosopher Paulo Freire said, "dialogue cannot exist without humility" (22). What we need to consider is the depth of connection required for building trustful relationships with teams and team members. Great leaders connect with people because they care about connecting with individuals.

WHEN GENUINE DIALOGUE DOES NOT HAPPEN

Understanding others means taking time to consider their interests, perspectives and needs. It starts with the desire to understand the other person, an openness and willingness to do so (mindset), and the generosity to show appreciation for them as individuals. Never underestimate the power and importance of an uninterrupted face to face "real-time" (synchronous) conversation, be it in the same room or via video. Such a conversation means going beyond the fact discussions and technical talk about tasks, which is all too common at work, and entering into genuine dialogue.

Technical dialogue is all about the exchange of facts. It is often simply focusing on informing others, with some clarification questions. **Discussions** focus more on winning, such as when we try to get our views across. There may be some emotional context linked to our personal position on a point, combined with fact-based evidence used to present ideas and concepts. Only **genuine dialogue** has the intention to establish a mutual relationship and occurs when participants have the other in mind. It is about exploring ideas together, it challenges us to listen to understand, not interrupt, hence avoiding assumptions and conflicts. It uses all elements of questioning, appreciating, recommending, informing and sharing vision and values (23). Such ability stems from well-developed communication skills and high emotional intelligence. Without high emotional intelligence it can feel un-authentic, false and one-directional.

In assessment centres we use an exercise to evaluate how leaders handle emotionally challenging situations. The participant has to discuss a deadline with an employee, yet the employee is visibly upset on arrival. Reactions vary considerably, from ploughing on regardless, to the employee being offered coffee. One particular candidate did not ask the employee to sit, did not ask them any questions and dismissed the upset employee with a clear "get it done by 4pm" yell.

In the feedback session we reviewed this highly insensitive behaviour with the participant to try to understand why someone would be so uncaring. The response – it's work, the job has to be done and personal problems should be left at home.

The issue?

Skill, mindset & presence – As a leader, results are only delivered with people and unhappy people cannot perform at their best and there is much data to correlate happy workers with increased productivity (160). This means a leader should and must care! In this example, the participant chose to ignore the employee's feelings and made the situation worse by demanding and shouting.

How to do better:

Meetings should always be respectful:

- Set the scene by welcoming people and asking them to sit down
- Connect before business by asking people how they are and responding to what is said, even if it means not discussing work tasks immediately
- Observe the non-verbal and have courage to pursue emotional conversations
- Tone down any desire to dominate or rush a conversation when putting the needs of others first is what may be required
- Show compassion: "I understand", "I care", "how can I help?"

USING EMOTIONAL INTELLIGENCE AND EMPATHETIC LISTENING TO CREATE EMPATHETIC DIALOGUE

Emotional intelligence or emotional quotient (EQ) as it is referred to when measured, is about learning to manage your own emotions and those of others for social success. Emotional competencies are proven to be crucial for effective communication as they predict how we deal with our own and other's feelings, anticipate reactions and understand how to be effective in social, stressful or emotional situations.

Strong emotional intelligence and balanced emotional competencies are essential for leaders.

Emotional intelligence is a learnt ability to engage, motivate and influence others and people with high emotional intelligence are usually successful in most things they do. Having high emotional intelligence ensures the right actions, as it enables people to choose their actions or communications for beneficial outcomes.

> *Emotional Intelligence is twice as important for excellent performance as technical skills and conventional IQ.*
>
> Daniel Goleman (11)

There are two sides of EQ, the intrapersonal elements are what goes on inside you, and the interpersonal, what goes on between you and other people. These two sides relate to balancing personal reactions and the mood or emotional subtleties of others. Strong "self" or intrapersonal intelligence is linked to sureness in one's self. Development of the "others" elements of interpersonal intelligence, also known as social intelligence, is paramount for connecting with others and building rapport as it includes empathy and social skills. This is the part that can bring care and compassion to the workplace by making others feel important. Through understanding other people, assumptions, judgements and stereotyping can be avoided and through treating people as valued individuals, people are motivated, engaged and more committed at work.

If we observe someone with high emotional intelligence, what will we see? Someone who:

- Never lets their temper get out of control
- Always speaks kindly to others and about others
- Listens to others
- Is easy to talk to
- Makes others feel relaxed, even important
- Has complete trust in their team and from their team
- Always makes careful, informed decisions

What someone with high emotional intelligence can do is think before they act or speak, even under stress. By doing so, they are preventing a quick, emotional response, evaluating a situation, and choosing a style of response and appropriate language for a better outcome. Critically, they are also able to behave and communicate well under stress or high-pressure work situations. For more on how to develop better emotional intelligence, see chapter 6.

THE REASON WHY WE HAVE 2 EARS, 2 EYES AND 1 MOUTH

When we start to consider what skills to develop to improve our one-to-one conversations, a good place to start is addressing the question "why do we have 2 ears, 2 eyes and 1 mouth"? The reason is, we should use them in that order and that ratio. As much as we may believe good communication comes from what we say, great communication comes from **listening and observing others**, in other words, putting others first.

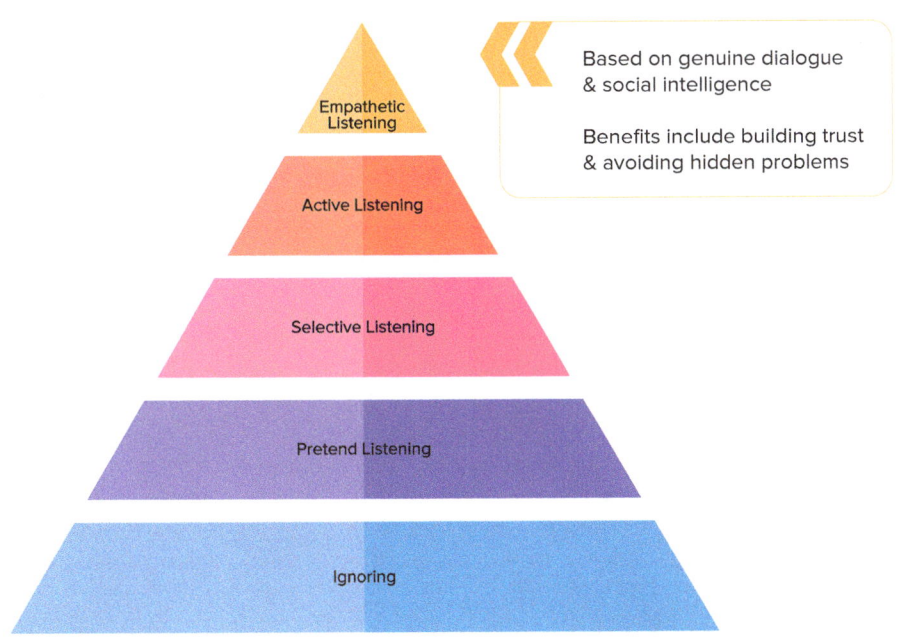

Figure 5: Five levels of listening

So why is listening so important? Well, listening makes people feel worthy, appreciated, interesting, and respected. In the business world it saves time and money by preventing misunderstandings because we learn more when we listen than when we talk. Even in our "love relationships", listening brings greater intimacy and parents listening to their kids helps build their self-esteem. Listening skills fuel our social, emotional and professional success and listening is a skill we can learn.

The highest level of listening, **empathetic listening** (24) comes with the desire to truly **understand** the other person before being understood yourself. It is paying attention to another person by emotionally identifying with them (empathy) and showing compassion to engage. It differs from connecting cognitively through "active listening", the technique to repeat back to the person what you think she or he said to make certain you understand. Empathetic listening is therefore about enhancing relationships with a stronger understanding of what is being conveyed, both intellectually and emotionally via structured listening and questioning.

To listen in an empathetic manner the following points can be used:

- Minimize internal and external distractions and **give your full attention**. Focus solely on what the speaker is saying - try not to think about what you are going to say next. Respond appropriately - show that you understand. Murmur and nod. Say words such as "Really," "Interesting," as well as more direct prompts: "What did you do then?" and "What was the response?"

- **Pay attention to body language** and the speaker's emotions. Do their words signal anger, frustration, pain, fear? Make and maintain eye contact. Are they fidgeting or adjusting their hand position? Pay attention to their body movement. All these signals will help you decipher their underlying feelings.
- **Ask neutral and thoughtful questions**. Don't make the conversation feel like an interrogation. Look the person in the eye and use a caring, gentle tone. Avoid questions that express an opinion or judgement or that could hurt or belittle. Ask specific yet open-ended questions about the particular issue, such as, "Would you mind sharing more about that?"
- Really **listen to replies** and be patient, even if you do not agree with them. Rephrase their words and encourage them to open up emotionally. Keep an open mind and try not to make assumptions about what the speaker is thinking. Avoid letting the speaker know how you handled a similar situation - unless they specifically ask for advice, assume they just need to talk it out.
- **Silence** is essential to empathetic listening. It adds depth and weight to a conversation. Though it may feel awkward at times, it provides space for the listener to think and the speaker to reflect on their reactions, current thinking and feelings, and consider solutions.
- Lastly, always **follow up**. It shows that you take the issue they raised seriously and have a stake in its successful outcome. It demonstrates that you care.

Empathetic listening can have many benefits (25). It can help untangle conflicts and solve disagreements. It also creates trust, validates the speaker and boosts their confidence. Teamwork and innovation are fostered when people listen to and understand each other and seek collaborative solutions.

THE POWER OF QUESTIONS IN COMMUNICATION

Listening is enhanced with skills in asking **powerful questions**. Questions start genuine dialogue, show interest and engage the other person and their brain. We are programmed to immediately look for answers to questions as an automatic brain function known as our predictive mind (26). When asking questions, you want to avoid getting yes / no answers, so avoid "can – do - did – have…". Open questions, that require more detailed answers, start with "why - how – who – what – where…".   Examples of questions that can make people stop and think differently can include:

- Why is this important to you?
- What is your thinking on this matter?
- What do you want the outcome to be?
- How will you make it happen?
- What is possible?
- What is the real issue?
- What matters most to you?
- How can I help?
- What could you/me/we have done better?
- What have you learnt from this?
- What would you do in my shoes?

> *The single biggest problem in communication is the illusion that it has taken place.*
>
> George Bernard Shaw (27)

Even when conversations go wrong or take an unexpected direction, questions can still be used. For example, if an idea of yours was dismissed, it is possible to use questions to **readdress topics** and continue dialogue, whilst still treating others with respect. By listening to the arguments of others, it acknowledges the legitimacy of their opinions. By accepting common points, neutral ground can be established, or you may even find ways to refocus on their interests. The point is how you approach such follow up to pave the way for further dialogue. Starting with "I would like to discuss the idea with you again" may get you a direct "absolutely not!", however, don't shout or get emotional or back down, change the tone. "I know you hated the idea as it may create a problem for you with …." Could be seen to acknowledge their strong feelings and show you have listened and are trying to see their view. "What is the concern you have about….?" is a way of reframing into understanding someone else's needs and getting more information and moving away from an argument. "Now I understand your reaction, yet we need to ……. Do you have any ideas about how I could achieve that without creating the …problem?" This can be seen to be moving around their position and promoting mutual cooperation and problem solving. Although you may not always achieve the outcome you want, asking in a professional way protects any relationship and improves understanding. It is also a vital skill for women in the workplace. In the book, "Women Don't Ask: Negotiation and the Gender Divide" (28), they suggest that women's socialization into passive roles is one of the reasons they do not succeed to higher management positions and they believe that having the skill to ask questions and readdress ideas in a constructive manner is a key learning point.

THE SIGNIFICANCE OF EMPATHY

Empathy is considered one of the most significant emotional competencies for personal success, as well as leadership success (29, 30, 31). It includes the ability to understand others' strengths and weak points, as well as their motives, and to identify with their needs and viewpoints. This means recognizing the feelings of others even when those feelings may not be obvious.

There are 3 parts of empathy:

- Cognitive empathy – knowing that you need to treat people individually so you can communicate in a way that others understand what you are saying (putting it in their terms)
- Emotional empathy – sensing or feeling what the other person is feeling (putting yourself in their shoes)

- Empathic concern – thinking, feeling and actually caring about the other person to genuinely say "I understand"

To show care however, you need to go to even further, to cultivate an attitude of loving kindness, or **compassion**, towards people. In this context, compassion incorporates the intention to act (12). It means communicating with the intention to connect with someone, to understand a person or situation, to make the situation better for them. EQ guru Goleman related this to "the caring system of the brain" and his view is that humanity needs compassion in order to survive (30). In his studies however, Goleman has found correlation between willingness to display empathy and compassion, with time constraints! Especially in the virtual world where the secret of connectedness and collaboration is trust, time and technology, the requirement for taking more time with people must be taken more seriously.

 **MINDSET WISDOM**

"Organizations are no longer built on force but on trust" (32)

- Trust is the precursor to positive engagement and organizational commitment.
- Trust is fostered through inspiring communication, positive influence and creating a safe environment in which others can thrive.
- Trust is allowing vulnerability, to speak openly about a mistake for example, because the expectation is that the other person will react in a positive way. Trust allows people to be honest with each other and to show their weaknesses as well as strengths, without fear of recrimination or abuse.

Chapter 3

IT'S HOW YOU TREAT OTHERS

Key knowledge

- Connecting with people means putting them first, and it takes effort, thought, and planning to get right
- Conversations go wrong when we keep going "our way" based on habit or belief we are right
- Leaders must avoid judgements or incorrect assumptions, especially when having difficult conversations

 Key models

- DISC model for adaptability
- Icebreakers for small talk
- TALK model for preparing messages balancing facts, feelings, guidance and relationships
- Power of thank you
- 3rd point technique for highlighting a problem
- ABC model when change is required
- 7 points to conflict resolution

 Impact

- Treating people as individuals and communicating in a way that they will be more re- ceptive to, not only shows care, but also desire to find a common way forward or joint resolution

Telling is not communicating. Informing on the next task is not communicating. Sending an email is not communication. These three examples may contain some element of attempted communication, yet for communication to be successful, people have to hear the right message, understand it and feel motivated to think differently and act differently as a result. Only when words have an impact is there success. Conversations are so often derailed because they are not based on dialogue and the speaker fails to consider the perspective of the listener.

MINDSET WISDOM

Stop pre-supposing what others want...

- Never assume that other people see things the same way or value the same things as you.
- Never judge others on personal outlooks.
- Perspective, the way we see something, has many and varied influencers (142). These can include, but are not limited or defined by, age, personality, motives, gender, background, culture, beliefs, even how you are feeling today...

From accepting that people are different and being open to engage in genuine dialogue, we are much better placed to learn what other's think, what they need and how to integrate their perspectives. It can however be very daunting to begin a conversation when you don't know how it will develop and this can also seem contrary to the idea of planning great communication. What you can do about it is have an arsenal of tools for considering how best to approach many common one-to-one situations that might arise. This includes, when and how to be more adaptable, how to engage in small talk, how to give feedback and especially, how to have difficult conversations.

HOW AGILE COMMUNICATION STYLES HELP TO GET YOUR POINT ACROSS

Interpersonal adaptability is also a desired emotional competence describing the willingness to adapt and modify behaviour without becoming personally invested or always having to do things your way. This is critical for adapting communication for individuals and situations. It must be in balance though; when too adaptable you can be perceived as lacking conviction and when too low, you will miss the range of behaviours to deal with different kinds of people or situations.

To be able to adapt or show more **versatility** in communication style, to ensure communication is as effective as possible, requires that you know your own natural style first.

Our communication style is an observable behaviour, and the image we create of ourselves, and may be different from how we believe we come across. Our first impressions may not be ideal! Communication can be unconscious or conscious. At times we knowingly adopt a different style when dealing with people as we actively aim to motivate and influence others or when attempting to behave as we believe we should, such as in presentations, meetings, interviews and when meeting people for the first time.

Angela is very sociable and loves her job as she has many opportunities to brainstorm with others and consider many creative ideas. She is aware however that not all people buy-in to her plans, especially Fred, who wants more details before he agrees to allocate resources.

The issue?

Skill – Angela is missing the ability to adapt her approach towards others. Though she may be happy with ambiguity and limited information, others require more structure and data before committing to projects.

How to do better:

Understanding yourself and others can mean valuing differences and being more willing to adapt:

- Understand your natural style and how you come across (try DISC)
- Consider the needs of others: Are they more direct, straight to business or more focused on small talk first? Do they want facts and details or the executive summary?
- Adapting styles and messages to provide information in the way others prefer it can increase influence and reduce friction

Many methodologies and tools are available to assess communication styles. One such example is DISC (33) which looks at observable behaviours and "how" people act. It is a simple approach measuring two dimensions: how people make decisions and whether people are introverts or extroverts. Four profiles then describe the characteristics and tendencies such people demonstrate naturally.

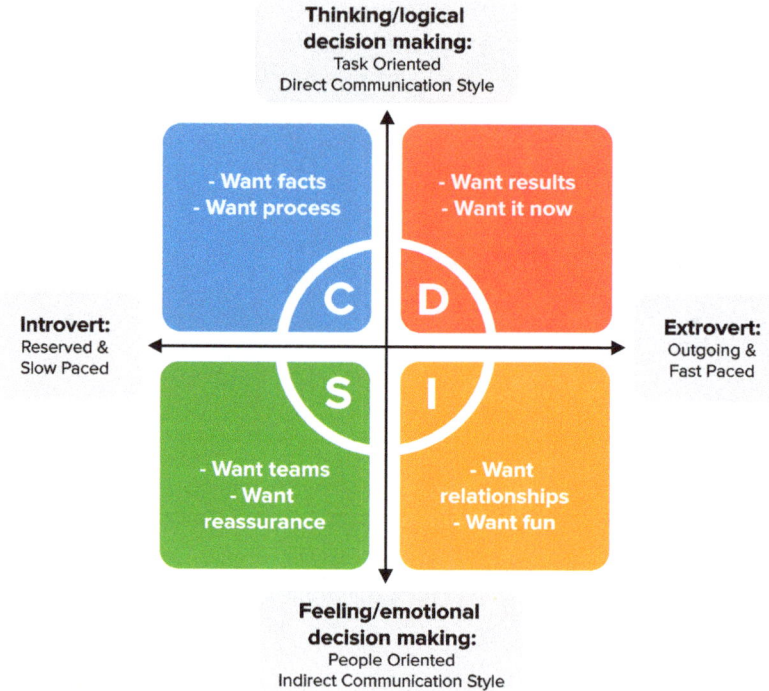

Figure 6: Communication styles from DISC methodologies (33)

D = dominance (red): Describes someone fast, task oriented, who wants results. This type of person is highly motivated by challenges and appears very proactive to solve problems quickly, hence decisive and communicating in a very direct, sometimes too telling manner.

I = influence (yellow): An extrovert and motivated by relationships. This person may be a strong networker, persuasive, optimistic and futuristic. Their style of communication is informal, wanting to connect to people before getting down to business. As they may like to discuss lots of ideas, they may appear unstructured to others.

S = steadiness (green): A quieter introverted person, motivated by calmer, more harmonious environments, a strong team player and one that needs more reassurance in communications. They are also dependable, supportive, loyal, systematic and a good listener, though not always willing to speak up in noisy environments.

C = compliance or conscientiousness (blue): Introverted thinkers motivated to act in environments of rules and procedures. As such they are detail oriented, analytical, accurate, and focused on quality. They want facts, are formal in communication yet need time to analyze to make rational choices. For others, this can be perceived as slow and hindering quick actions.

Such a tool is useful to explore personal behavioural or communication styles, to learn to recognize the communication style of others and then learn to adapt and blend styles for more effective communication and relationships. Such interpersonal adaptability shows inclination to adapt to different people and circumstances and modify behaviour to relate to others better. It is not about being un-authentic, it is about having a toolbox of skills and versatility to act in a manner that the other person will be more receptive to. For example, if someone is naturally more of an influencer (yellow), they will need to communicate in a more direct and specific manner and deliver more facts to a blue type person to engage them. It is planning how the content of the message can be more appropriate for the other person, as well as the manner of delivery, especially the speed and body language. Another example: a dominant red will need to tone down their speech and be more reassuring and allow thinking time when they are trying to get a "green" person onboard with a new idea. Pushing for a quick answer will never work in this instance! For more on how to develop better adaptive communication, such as by applying DISC, see chapter 7.

THE IMPORTANCE OF INFORMAL CHAT OR SMALL TALK

One of the most difficult aspects of being a leader, especially a senior leader, is that people look to you for input, direction, even reassurance. This means being aware of "being on show" much of the time. It also means being able to chat and engage in positive and stimulating small talk with anyone at any time and being appropriate, especially adapting, in these more ad hoc situations. Such informal or casual communication is spontaneous, can be broad and outside of regular formalities. The purpose of informal communication can include sharing of information, establishing personal contacts or making friendships. It can be supplementing official channels so therefore has to be considered in its content. When it happens with someone you don't know very well, for example in the coffee shop queue, then it often becomes polite conversation about unimportant things – small talk.

Never underestimate the impact of small talk however as albeit brief, it leaves an impression of you in the eyes of the other person. So, though many start by discussing the weather or the latest sports news, you could try more thought-provoking questions that can't be answered with a simple yes or no. You may learn about other people or get surprising insights. By inviting people to speak, share ideas or share an interesting story, it also demonstrates you care what they think, and it starts to build rapport. It makes them feel more important and acknowledged when you give someone your undivided attention, even for just one minute. A short conversation may in fact brighten up someone else's day. Key is finding appropriate topics, both for you and the other person and also having the courage to start a chat even when you feel uncomfortable, as it is about making the other person feel more comfortable.

Here are some "small talk" openers, or icebreakers, that we like (34):

Work:
- How did you become a [job title]?
- What surprises you most about your job?
- If you weren't working here, what would you be doing right now?

Entertainment:
- Are you reading any good books right now?
- Are there any apps on your phone that you can't live without?
- Do you have any podcast suggestions for my commute?

Travel:
- What's the best "hidden gem" around here?
- Where's the last place you travelled? What did you do there?
- What's the next trip you have planned?

Life Story:
- Where did you live before this? What are the biggest differences you see?
- What did you think you were going to be growing up?
- Do you have any hidden talents or surprising hobbies?
- Who's the most important role model or mentor you've had in your life?
- What's the best piece of advice you've ever received?

HOW TO PLAN MORE EFFECTIVE FORMAL COMMUNICATION USING THE 4-SIDES OR TALK MODE

Communication is a process and should be understood as such. It has steps in order to achieve a particular outcome or goal. In the business world, we are familiar with goal setting, the development of a plan designed to motivate and guide others towards a desired outcome. This structured cognitive approach can help shape the effectiveness of communication. If we focus specifically on internal communications between a leader and team member, **goals or desired outcomes** can include (9):

- Informing or setting expectations about tasks or projects
- Showing appreciation for contributions or outcomes, or reassuring, even comforting people in the workplace when required
- Understanding employees, their needs, strengths, ideas or concerns

- Questioning and discussing business topics, seeking solutions or decisions together
- Giving feedback or conveying negative messages, along with possible solutions and consequences when performance or results are not met
- Sharing a vision or re-positioning or changing direction

The challenge with communication is always whether it was received correctly and the right actions resulting for the defined goals. It is not always evident that the receiver understands the message from the sender exactly the way that it was meant. With the relationship aspect of communication so critical, communicators must understand this and take steps to avoid misunderstandings. It means communication should be well planned, including the message itself, the format or channel, even the timing.

Stefan is a new manager and has instigated weekly meetings with each of his team members. He acknowledges that communication feels more difficult when his employees don't listen to his directions on how to complete tasks properly. As an expert, Stefan knows how to do things properly.

The issue?

Mindset – It is always better to focus on results than methods as other people will have new ideas and new approaches. Never assume your way is the best.

Skill – With all employees, it is always essential to prepare conversations, especially if they are likely to be difficult, such as redefining expectations or giving challenging feedback. What is important to note is that the relationship aspect is possibly by far the most important to determine how the content is understood (remember the second axiom - content is what we say but our relationship determines how we understand meaning).

How to do better:

Focusing on results is a key aspect of effective management (35):

- Discuss and agree goals to motivate through common direction, rather than micro-managing the how and what

Prepare for meetings whenever possible:

- Understand your goal, your key content, your relationship and use a model to prepare a structured message, such as TALK

To complement our understanding of the balance of relationships and content in communication, it is important to consider that every message has four facets, though emphasis may not be placed equally on each. The four sides of a message are facts, self-revelation by the sender, appeal to the receiver, and finally the relationship (4).

From the senders' perspective, the **factual** level (i) contains statements or information which are part of the news to be communicated. In **self-revealing** (ii), the sender consciously or unconsciously expresses something about themselves, their motives, values, emotions. The **appeal** (iii) contains the guidance, advice, instruction or effect that the sender is seeking. In the **relationship** (iv) element the sender is conveying how they get along with the receiver, even what they think of them. This can be in formulation of the message, body language or intonation and can express respect, friendliness, disinterest, contempt etc.

The challenge is the interpretation or how the receiver "hears" the message sent! From the factual information element, the receiver "hears" whether the message fulfils criteria of truth (true/untrue) or relevance (relevant/irrelevant) and the completeness (satisfying/something has to be added). From the sender's self-revelation, the receiver perceives which information about the sender is often hidden in the message. As the relationship layer expresses how the sender gets along with the receiver, indicators to the receiver will include you-statements suggesting what the sender thinks of them, and we-statements, how the two get along. Depending on which message the receiver "hears", they feel either depressed, accepted or patronized. A good communication is distinguished by communication with mutual appreciation. Finally, on the appeal side, the receiver asks, "what should I do, think or feel now?"

This all sounds complicated, yet every layer can be misunderstood individually. The emphasis on the four sides can be meant differently and also be understood differently. So, the sender can stress the appeal of the statement and the receiver can mainly receive the relationship part of the message. This is one of the main reasons for misunderstandings.

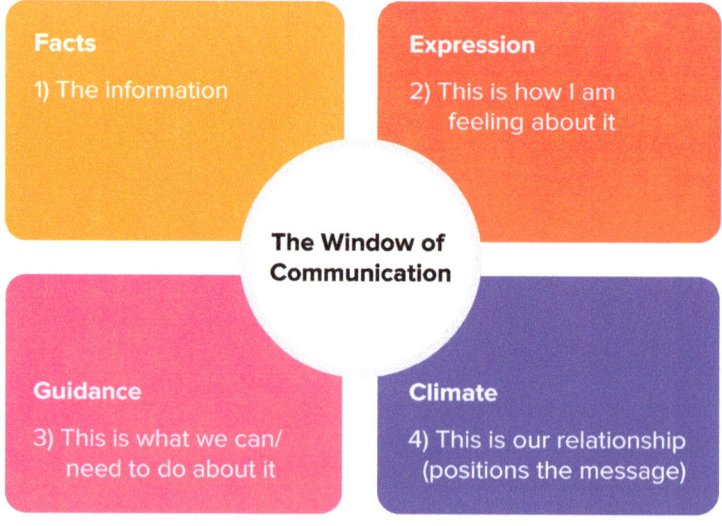

Figure 7: The TALK Model (36)

To make this more thinking tangible, let's look at the TALK model which is an application of this theory (36) and how it can be used to plan better communication, either one-to-one or for a team.

> A sales manager needs to communicate that the company has a big problem because revenues are down. What is better? To simply say our revenues are down and demand action, or be more considered and use the TALK framework?
> 1. Being clear on the facts, what information or message needs to be conveyed; for example, sales are down at 80% of plan and targets will be missed unless actions are implemented now. Specific, yet non-aggressive, non-judgemental.
> 2. The sales manager's expression or feeling on the situation; for example, they can reveal that they are concerned the team will miss commission or bonus payments if gaps are not filled.
> 3. Appealing to the receiver by giving inputs shows specific guidance, such as let's look at focusing on segments a, b or c.... Let's bring in resources to achieve x,y,z......
> 4. Finally, the overall message can be encased much better when solidarity is shown in difficult situations, for example, "we are in this together, as a team we can all focus to complete this on time". This is framing the relationship between sender and receiver.

Hopefully this highlights that such an empathetic and specific communication is more engaging and more useful! This preparation can be used for meetings, phone calls and video meetings. What this also does is open more difficult conversations and allows the sender to communicate known information. It may not however be the best model for unknown situations, that goes back to the power of questions and empathetic listening that need to be used in open conversation.

HOW TO ACHIEVE UNDERSTANDING AND COMMITMENT

Beyond relaying information or facts, the process of communication needs to work smoothly to affect the receiver or cause a reaction. The process also requires checks for understanding and acceptance. As it is a process, feedback at each step or phase can avoid failure. In the case that a step or phase fails, it must be repeated.

Figure 8: Phases of conversations

The following phases can be considered when entering a conversation or genuine dialogue:

- Opening of communication is the **first phase** of welcoming, setting the scene or creating context, defining why the conversation is taking place. Content can include setting goals and agreeing how the conversation or meeting will flow. The aim of this phase should be building or confirming the relationship aspect, even creating a feeling of safety for participants. It's all about trust.
- **Phase two** is assessing the situation or needs of the person or topic. Dialogue is key here as the two-way element to relay information, ask questions, listen and integrate new perspectives. The aim is therefore to exchange facts or information in order to fully understand personal needs or the situation.
- **Phase three** begins to address the issues and seek solutions together. Through continued dialogue, objections can be reviewed, more information may be needed, and ideas, options, alternatives and consequences explored. If real understanding is achieved, alignment of next steps can occur.
- **Phase four** is commitment, an active step to obtain feedback and agreement on a win-win outcome. Assuming buy-in is very risky, so both verbal and non-verbal affirmations should be sought – watch for the body language and specifically ask if there is agreement for action. Remember personal commitment must also be demonstrated.
- Finally, **phase five**, ending the communication or meeting is once again being responsive to people, acknowledging, respecting and concluding with a sense of comfort which leaves the door open for further discussions, in other words, securing the relationship.

If a conversation is conducted according to these phases, chances of achieving commitment and buy-in to goals will increase. Even in virtual settings the phases remain and especially when underpinned by trust, appropriate time investment and tools such as video calls, the likelihood of all participants leaving with a positive feeling is higher!

MINDSET WISDOM

- **Honouring self-esteem allows for successful communication**
- **Belittling self-esteem disturbs communication**

It is important to remember that communication must consider the feelings of participants. Communication has impact on the self-esteem of others. If self-esteem is hurt, the communication quality suffers, and the sender is responsible for the effect of the communication on the receiver. Optimal communication increases the self-esteem of participants and only by honouring self-esteem is a real win-win achieved. This once again links back to relationship aspects and avoiding misuse of power to achieve positive influence (37, 38)

THE IMPORTANCE OF FEEDBACK

Surveys have shown many people do not show high self-awareness (39) nor self-reflection, yet many teachings related to emotional intelligence indicate this insight is fundamental for personal change and growth (9, 11, 29, 40, 41). Self-awareness is having a conscious knowledge of yourself, including the ability to form an accurate self-concept and understand the impact you have on others. Self-reflection is fundamental in considering your own role in situations and makes self-responsibility possible. A key question is "how can you help others improve self-awareness"? One way is through feedback, especially important when someone has a blind spot or a lack of awareness of a strength or development area that can be seen by others. Critical to feedback is that it is constructive and focused on boosting someone else's confidence and ability.

Figure 9: Summary of three types of feedback (42)

The first type of feedback is appreciation. This is a form of recognition and motivation and should be given for who someone is and what they do well. It should not be combined with an improving or learning message. Secondly, evaluation relates to performance and part of the assessment and performance review managers undertake during annual appraisals for example. The third type of feedback is when **coaching to improve performance and growth**. This is where extra care should be taken because simply telling people what we think of their performance does not help and telling them how we think they should improve can hinder learning (43). Be very aware of the help or advice that has not been asked for, or taking over when someone is trying to learn, or over-explaining. All this second guessing is smothering and patronising.

Part 1: The Real-Life Work Situations (and Models to Help)

Alex watched Maria struggle to faciltate a project meeting. Immediately afterwards, Alex spoke with Maria to share observations and point out what went wrong. "I would have handled it like...." Began Alex. "You allowed people to talk for too long. You should have shut down the discussion much sooner" continued Alex.

The issue?

Mindset – Telling someone how you would have done it better is not good feedback for coaching. Starting from your own perspective causes errors in how you rate the performance of others and is biased by your own assumptions.

How to do better:

Immediate feedback is important, yet the focus should be seeking to enhance abilities:

- Ask questions first – "how do you think that went?", "why do you think there was no agreement" … It is essential the other person recognizes the reality of the problem and is able to recognize their role in it
- From acknowledgment of the problem, questions can move on to probe what options can be considered for making changes and what the person will do to develop
- Key is building from what went well and then what could be even better

To **give insightful coaching-based feedback** (44, 45) that is more likely to be accepted, the receiver must recognize themselves in the feedback. It therefore helps to be specific and concrete, with examples. It must be based upon personal observations, not interpretations or valuation. It should also be useful for the receiver, seemingly valuable for reinforcing and developing of strengths, not focused on what they can't do. It should never be targeted towards unachievable brilliance but rather on being even better at something. Finally, feedback works best within a trusting relationship. However, it is important to remember that receivers also need to be open to receive. Feedback must be presented as a gift and if it is an unwelcome gift, the giver must also accept this.

IT'S NOT ALL BAD IN THE OFFICE…SHOWING APPRECIATION

Showing appreciation is not only excellent feedback it is also one of the key forms of communication necessary to relate to others (9), and it's also a fun part of communicating. According to Steven Covey, author of "The 7 Habits of Highly Effective People", "next to survival, the greatest need of a human being is… to be understood, affirmed, validated and appreciated" (46). Further research has also shown that employees are most satisfied and motivated through recognition of performance and achievement. However, formal recognition can sometimes be perceived as predictable, routine and impersonal (47). What works better is personalized encouragement and recognition expressed from the heart.

Feeling genuinely appreciated lifts people up, makes people feel safe, which frees them up to do their best work. When personal value feels at risk, worry becomes preoccupying, which drains and diverts energy from creating value (48). Feeling valued also helps avoid conflict.

To show appreciation, there are **two very powerful words: Thank You.** Two very powerful words and as rewards, certainly inexpensive. Studies into appreciation and the use of "thank you" does show dramatic impact and personal congratulations rank at the top of motivators by many employees (47). So, spreading thanks really can make a difference! This can also be applied every day – even using names in an email "Dear Fred", rather than simply opening with a statement, helps connect. Acknowledging work received by email with a simple "thanks" not only reassures message receipt, it again shows simple appreciation for the work done.

HIGHLIGHTING A PROBLEM USING THE 3RD POINT TECHNIQUE

On the flip side, an often-daily occurrence can be having to highlight errors, problems or areas of concern related to tasks, processes, complaints or even people. The wrong way is "you have a problem". This is made even worse if we use intense eye contact at the same time. The message being sent is "you are the problem".

Eye contact helps to display interest and confidence. It is considered appropriate to maintain eye contact for 50% of the time while speaking and 70% while listening and once you establish eye contact, hold it for 4-5 seconds. Your eyes are a way of building a connection with the other person and building trust. However, when having difficult conversations, no matter how professionally delivered, the risk is hurting the feelings of the recipient when face-to-face. A better approach is to introduce a neutral "3rd point" (49).

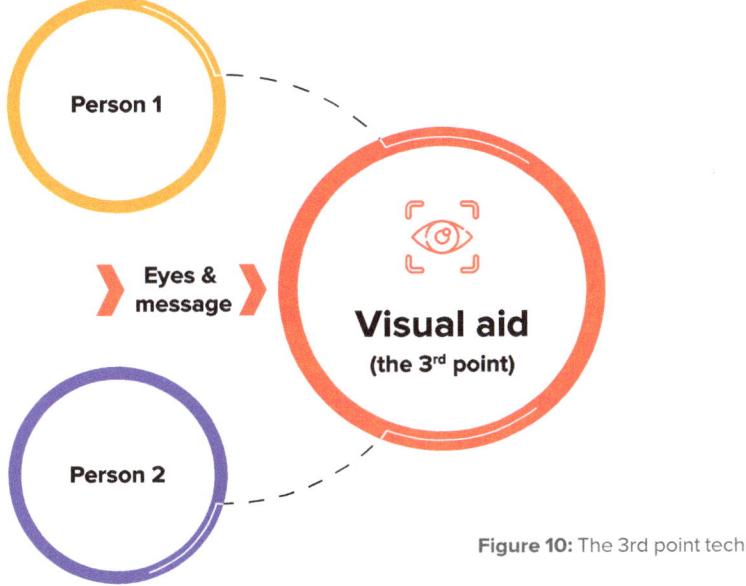

Figure 10: The 3rd point technique

With your eyes and your message directed at the 3rd point, such as the data to highlight the issues, the 3rd point deflects the personal component and makes the conversation more objective. The recipient is not directly confronted, intimidated, or losing face. With both parties looking down, the interaction is not person-centred. By pointing to the 3rd point you can say "this is the problem", not "you are the problem". Imagine a doctor using an x-ray to show a broken bone by pointing out the break specifically. Talking to the 3rd point in this way is very useful for negative issues. As a counterbalance, remember to talk to the person about good news, such as the doctor addressing the patient directly and saying, "you are well".

HOW TO DEAL WITH UNDER-ACHIEVEMENT AND INSPIRE CHANGE

A key task of a leader is to convey confidence in employees' abilities. This includes encouraging and supporting employees, making suggestions for improvements, and addressing ideas openly. One of the challenging aspects can be handling under-achievement when required in a constructive manner. Being overly "nice" and not addressing issues is not helping others in the long run.

Alex requested a meeting with an employee to discuss yet another customer complaint. The email that prompted the meeting simply said "your employee was so rude we are taking our business elsewhere".

Alex handed the employee a copy of the email and demanded an explanation. The conversation quickly escalated into an argument until Alex called a halt.

The issue?

Skill — It is very clearly a manager's responsibility to address issues, however, this is where most stop. Most do not have the skill to lead the conversation to an appropriate outcome which goes beyond the problem and seeks solutions, and in a constructive manner that avoids the employee getting defensive or argumentative.

How to do better:

- Firstly, never assume you know the cause of the problem
- Secondly, never confront others based on hearsay or get emotional in the discussion
- Thirdly, plan and follow the 3-step approach, ABC.

ABC is an easy to remember and useful tool for preparing constructive discussions where new expectations need to be communicated.

A: Address the problem – It is a leader's job to put issues on the table! So, open the meeting and quickly state your concerns about the problem, be specific. Use facts to describe the situation clearly and calmly. Use evidence and personal observations to describe behaviours. Never refer to others or hearsay as you immediately get distracted by the who said what argument.

B: Bridge to the employee – This means creating a respectful or emotional connection with the employee by acknowledging what they are good at, giving positive inputs and then asking open questions to understand their perspective on the current problem. You need the employee to open up and this will only happen through a trusting and safe dialogue. Once they are able to share their views, you can review facts and generate alternative solutions together. You can even show how you can help them.

C: Consequences – This is the part many leaders miss yet it is vital to be clear on what you expect, so be specific on the change required or the new behaviour that needs to be seen. Agree on what each person will do to resolve the problem and next steps. Be clear on how you will monitor process and be clear on the consequences if progress or change is not demonstrated by the agreed time. Consequences do not have to mean you will fire them or other direct punishments. They can include highlighting the impact on the customer, project or business results. For many committed employees, once the impact of a problem is highlighted, the motivation of purpose or shared goals can be enough to stimulate learning and improvement.

MINDSET WISDOM

A growth mindset is better suited for learning and personal development
- A growth mindset is associated with people who see their abilities as learned traits which can be developed.
- Such people are open to challenges and new experiences, see failure as a chance to learn and are receptive to feedback and coaching. They are persistent in the face of setbacks and see effort as the path to mastery.
- Opposite is a fixed mindset that can result in people plateauing, giving up and feeling threatened by the success of others (50).)

HOW TO IDENTIFY AND RESOLVE CONFLICTS

Conflict is a serious disagreement often arising from a clash of interests, objectives or values. Conflict is way beyond simple differences of opinion, and it can be caused by poor communication, mistrust, attitude, lack of honesty or insubordination. It is also associated with an escalating process and in severe cases, 3rd parties are often needed for resolution.

There are 7 principles to seeking a resolution (51):

1. Seek common ground
2. Focus on the problem
3. Objectify the situation – keep emotions out
4. Acknowledge positions – the set outcomes each party believes they want
5. Acknowledge and focus on needs – the interests or wishes of each party
6. Validate feelings – to show respect and understanding
7. Listen empathetically

The ideal outcome is collaboration when there is desire to cooperate all round. This can be achieved with an integrative solution when both sets of concerns are too important to be compromised. It can include merging insights from people with different perspectives, gaining commitment by incorporating others' concerns and working through hard feelings which may have been interfering with the relationship. It requires that all people are valued equally and treated with respect.

But how? It starts from acceptance that this is not a competition or adversarial contest, but a **collaborative dialogue** with two goals - issue-related goals and relationship goals.

Techniques to facilitate the dialogue include:

- Ask "diagnosing" questions – "what problem do you have" or "what problem does this create for you"?
- Share information about your own interests or needs
- Unbundle the issues – "is there a way for you to ... if I ...."
- Brainstorm about possible solutions rather than defending established positions – "how can we both get ...."

Resolution often comes from **understanding needs** (interests/wishes) not positions (set outcomes / wants):

Example 1: The window

Two men are arguing in the office. One wants the window open and the other wants it closed. They bicker about how much to leave it open – a crack or halfway? No solution satisfies them both.

Enter a woman. She asks one why he wants the window open – "to get some fresh air". She asks the other why he wants it closed – "to avoid the draft". She walks into the corridor and opens a window wide, bringing fresh air in, without a draft.

Example 2: The lemon

Two celebrity chefs are preparing dinner together. Opening the fridge, they discover there is only one lemon and they both say they want a lemon to finish their dishes.

What happens next when each argues he should get the lemon? The chefs argue their position, but what are the options?

- A disruptive solution? One chef gets the lemon.
- A compromise? Cut the lemon in half.
- Or understand the interests of each chef by asking what the chefs really need.

What if one chef needs the rind for a cake and the other needs the juice for a marinade? If they know each other's interests, they may get a better solution!

HOW TO BUILD RELATIONSHIPS EVEN IN THE VIRTUAL WORLD?

In virtual environments, the challenges and barriers to effective communication are even higher and require extra effort. It is easier when people are in the same room, yet virtual communication and connecting to employees in our digital age is ever more paramount. How best to communicate when people are not physically present means new skills such as digital competencies, and more considered message creation to avoid uncertainty or misinterpretation. More time is needed for discussion, along with more willingness to get to know individuals, their needs and their styles. It all comes down to more efforts to build trust. When considering the axioms of communication, there may be hidden reactions and missing body language clues plus appropriate consideration of power that all have to be factored in. In the digital age, leaders need to expand beyond face-to-face leadership, into successful leadership of remote and virtual teams, including home workers.

Success in life only comes from the willingness to reach out to others and to build bridges. Yet it is even more difficult when you can't see the other side.

Anonymous (52)

Part 1: The Real-Life Work Situations (and Models to Help)

The 2020 COVID-19 pandemic experience accelerated the existing, yet slower, shift to virtual working and highlighted significant challenges of workplaces becoming more distant. The combination of digital tools and simple creativity did unlock all sorts of new experiences: from virtual parties, to virtual museum tours and art viewings, to virtual team building like virtual happy hour drinks. Such events created shared experiences and identity within a team to mediate the effects of physical separation. Highly effective virtual communication also requires digital tools and creative thinking to achieve a feeling of cooperation and interconnectedness. If great communication is all about showing someone else that they are important, then making virtual communication more personal is key. For more details, see chapter 4.

SUMMARY OF CONNECTING AND INFLUENCING ONE-TO-ONE

Concept Level	Audience scenario	Goal	Communication Characteristics			Models	Additional virtual considerations
			Skills	Mindset	Presence		
Relationship building	Individuals in one-to-one settings	Dialogue & motivation	- Sharing ideas & information - Creating empathetic dialogue - Giving feedback - Appreciating - Addressing issues - Handling conflict	- Trust - Showing care - Openness to differences - Challenging assumptions	- Positive body language - Giving attention - Investing time	- DISC - Ice-breakers - TALK - Thank you - 3rd Point - ABC - 7 points to conflict resolution	- A face-to-face feel - Use of technology

Chapter 4:

THE TROUBLE WITH GROUPS

Key knowledge

- Group work requires significant planning, structure and understanding to achieve active participant from all parties
- Communication in groups needs more focus on audience needs, to be inspiring and relevant
- More virtual teamwork requires extra investment in trust, time and technology

 Key models

- Conscious communication styles when working in groups
- Balanced engagement to guide, share or facilitate
- WHY model to inspire
- BRIEF model to structure memorable messages
- Connecting and Influencing despite distance

 Impact

- Ensuring all voices are heard, new ideas are sought and collaborative problem solving occurs leading to increased creativity, innovation and performance

In this chapter we will start to explore the challenges and solutions for communication and influence within group settings, the middle level of the communication and influence model (see figure 11). The focus shifts to collaboration and the target audience is a team or group of people. Key is achieving participation from all parties and in the virtual environment, consideration needs to be on how to ensure live and lively interactions from all. It is also important to note that groups mean more people and direct influence begins to diminish. The type of communication also varies. Immediate, **real-time or synchronous communication** can occur in team meetings for example, to gather broad insights, discuss ideas and engage all parties in collaborative decision making. **Asynchronous (delayed) communication** also needs to be applied as it is great to allow people to engage in work topics at their own pace and reflect, add inputs and respond when appropriate. Such availability is also essential for working across different time zones and to provide flexibility for working when/where is most appropriate. The tools and technologies need to be in place however, to facilitate such sharing and active co-working. This means utilizing communication skills and new digital competencies to have appropriate collaboration strategies and effective implementation.

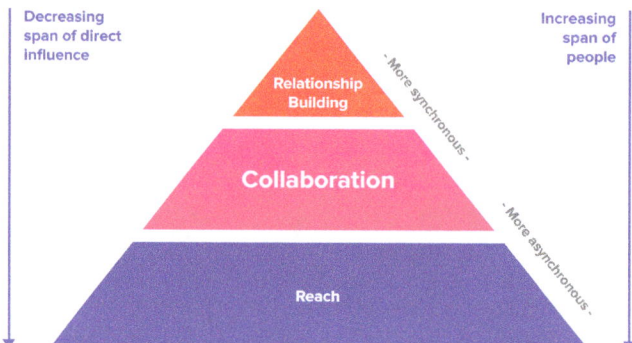

Figure 11: Ability to communicate and maintain influence at all levels is required in business

Teamwork is the collaborative effort of a group of people to achieve a common goal or to complete a task in the most effective and efficient way. With virtual teams and remote workers becoming increasingly important in today's fast-paced, digitally interlinked and ever-changing world, collaboration is also changing. Virtual teamwork across different locations offers employees and leaders great opportunities for flexibility, diversity and motivation; yet, there are considerable challenges of distance that must be overcome. Even with distance, when we begin to consider such communication and collaboration, it is essential to remember that achieving influence is still important, necessitating trust building, as well as investing time in people and leveraging the right technology.

> *Inclusion is not simply about proximity. It is about intentionally planning for the success of all.*
>
> Tim Villegas (53)

MINDSET WISDOM

The mindset to include everyone for collaboration has 3 parts:

- **Active inclusion** - includes time and willingness to integrate everyone and actively include all team members. This is true not only for meetings to inform but also taking time to ask the team for input and empower them get involved and take initiative. It shows the team really is in this together.
- **Avoid assumptions** – as these limit connections. For example, even when the team vision and goals are clear, talk about them a lot! Talk about personal values, how you work, how to find information etc ... it is easy to forget what's going on in bigger groups.
- **Open door** – for the informal as well as formal communication. Let people know how to reach you.

Before we explore communication and collaboration within teams, let's consider the **traits of high-performing teams** to be clear on what we are aiming for (54). For teams to function well over time they share purpose and direction, have motivating goals and all members understand their roles and are committed to joint success. Teams require authority for decision making and include diverse talents for expertise and insights. The team must have a willingness to support and trust one another, and finally, communication is essential, and this needs to be in all directions, formats and mixing the formal and informal.

 Angela invited the team for their first zoom event. However it did not go as she planned. Even when she began to introduce all participants the interruptions started. When she asked questions, everyone was talking all at once and then there were the technical challenges when connections were lost and background noises took over....

 The issue?

Skill – Any form of meeting, either in one room or remotely, requires solid facilitation skills and meeting rules. Any virtual meeting requires even more digital skills to avoid frustrations.

 How to do better:

- In the physical world it's not usually technology that is the problem but poor planning and preparation. Top issues are no agenda, off topic distractions, lack of preparation, no decisions or outcomes.
- In the virtual world, sophisticated technological tools are required for more effective virtual communication, yet team performance depends on how people use these technologies, not on the technologies themselves (55).

THE IMPORTANCE OF "THE MEETING" FOR TEAM PERFORMANCE

The meeting is actually a key management tool, alongside reports, budgets, job assignments and appraisals (35). Meetings serve functions (56) such as defining a group or team, revising and updating what is known by the group, agreeing group goals and understanding individual contributions, decision making and enabling the leader to shape the way the group succeeds. Though meetings may vary by size, frequency or composition, common elements of successful meetings are:

- A clear goal or objective for the meeting
- Reason for who is present
- Documentation, either for preparation or follow up
- An agenda, structure and rules, including who is responsible for leading the meeting
- An outcome and actions

In today's world there is also the choice of how to host a meeting, whether it be physical or digital and there are advantages of both the physical and the virtual/digital meeting (57).

Face-to-face meetings bring energy and allow physical interaction and human connections. For example, simple gestures such as handshakes are related to expressiveness and research has shown that a handshake reveals personality traits and is an opportunity to make a favourable first impression (58). This is obviously lost in the digital space. Decision making can also be more effective in face-to-face meetings due to the ease of integrating others, especially quieter team members. Body language can also be observed, and more open discussion of different perspectives, options, alternatives and consequences is possible in small physical groups.

ELEMENT	PHYSICAL	DIGITAL	QUICK THOUGHTS
Energy	+	-	Energy is - almost by definition - higher "in the room"
Human Connection	+	-	No comparison. Physical trumps digital massively
Decision making	+	-	Decisions can be easy, but alignment is harder digitally
Travel Time	-	+	For some organizations, massive time is saved here
Cost	-	+	Overall cost is lower - sometimes much lower
Logistics	-	+	Distributed instead of centralised. Simpler by far
Scheduling	-	+	Easier, due to less time loss overall
Notes	-	+	Easier both individually and collectively
Breakout Sessions	-	+	Faster and smoother, and with zero logistics issues
Q&A	-	+	Often less boring due to ability to zone out gracefully

Figure 12: The advantages of physical and virtual meetings (57)

Remote meetings on the other hand can be more cost efficient and travel time eliminated. Also good for the environment. Scheduling can be easier for remote meetings and tools can be used for sharing documents, making notes, running breakout sessions, even brainstorming by using white board solutions. It can also be seen to be an advantage to gracefully step back in remote meetings when your part is done. Key is making either format as successful as possible.

THE INFLUENCE OF PSYCHOLOGY ON TEAM PERFORMANCE

Despite the obvious use of meetings in business and even with the mindset for inclusion to make collaborations work, groups need to be carefully understood because there are fundamental differences between individual and group mentalities. Leaders also need to role model good behaviour.

In a recent workshop, the event began well as participants were open, willing to ask lots of questions and share positive experiences. However, half way through, a senior manager decided to vocalize his opinions. He started to interrupt other participants, showed judgement of their inputs and was cynical of examples. The entire dynamic changed and earlier contributors then remained silent and those that did speak up tried to distance themselves from his comments and started to use the word "toxic" in their examples.

The issue?

Presence – Any senior leader must be aware of the power of their position and signals sent by their language, tone, body language and judgement towards others. In this example, the senior leader demonstrated disregard for others, lack of empathy and rudeness. Not only did he try to dominate the workshop and limit the learning of others, as a role model, he was also showing that such poor behaviour was acceptable.

How to do better:

A senior leader should never intimidate or belittle the inputs of others, especially in a public setting. Instead:

- Show respect and due regard for the feelings, wishes, or rights of others – this is the basis of trust
- Seek understanding and engagement through questions in an empathetic and kind manner – never shout or dismiss or bully
- Foster group cohesion by reinforcing a safe environment in which people can speak up without fear of ridicule – role model desired behaviour, be fair, build esteem, value differences, or otherwise, shut up!

This example of poor behaviour, lack of integrity and lack of care for others' feelings is compounded because such a leader is also saying this is acceptable behaviour! Such a starting point will always encourage poor group dynamics.

There are however other reasons why teamwork does not always go to plan and let's start by looking at an example of group phenomenon known as **bystander apathy**, a phenomenon concerning people's likeliness to help in an emergency situation (59).

Why doesn't everyone step forward?

Someone else will do something...   Don't want to behave differently...

According to Bystander Apathy or the Bystander Effect, the greater the number of other people present, the less likely any one of them are to act. Why? There are two reasons (59):

1. When we are in a crowd, we assume that someone else will do something
2. No one wants to be the person who is behaving differently

When we translate this to business and meetings, we can see the risk of **dilution of responsibility** in groups and secondly, the influence of social pressure that it is "ok" not to act when others don't. So, what is all this about? Human beings are pack animals and as such, we are driven by desire to belong. However, we are also subject to many unconscious biases. Group phenomena consider the behaviours of individuals that often change in a group setting.

Joining groups satisfies the individual need to belong, defines self and social identity, gains information and helps achieve goals that might elude individuals alone. However, for all these positives, negatives also arise. Though people who are accepted members of a group tend to feel happier and more satisfied, should they be rejected by a group, they feel unhappy, helpless, and depressed. Studies of **ostracism**, the deliberate exclusion from groups, indicate this experience is highly stressful and can lead to depression, confused thinking, and even aggression (60). This can also diminish identity and self-esteem.

Further negatives include, **polarization**, whereby the group is divided into opposing sub-groups; or **scapegoating**, the singling out a person or sub-group for unmerited blame. Finally, **groupthink**, the drive for consensus is an enormous hindrance to creativity and innovation as nothing new comes to the table once groupthink sets in.

However, effective teams are, in most cases, **cohesive groups** (61). Group cohesion is the integrity, solidarity, social integration, or unity of a group. Members of cohesive groups like each other and the group and they also are united in their pursuit of collective, group-level goals. To avoid the negative aspects of group phenomena, a leader must understand the risks and overcome such potential pitfalls.

HOW TO STOP GROUPTHINK

In the context of communication, collaborative work and active participation, with the intent on performance, achievement and innovation, the key phenomenon to overcome is groupthink. Overcoming this is essential for a productive, creative and critical thinking atmosphere.

Groupthink is an **exaggerated striving for harmony and agreement**, especially in very homogeneous groups (62). Stress, bad communication or missing neutrality of the leader are other important aspects and overall, this endangers realistic assessments and decision-making. Groupthink can be recognized when a group overestimates itself, decisions are not being questioned and not all relevant information is gathered, especially when the information is not positive. A further symptom is the missing reflection of different options and the missing evaluation and review of the final solution.

Groupthink is not consequent for every team, in every situation. But even in teams that usually work together very well, groupthink can happen, especially in stress situations caused by external factors like new customer demands thrown on to a team in limited time frames or sometimes when people can't be bothered to engage in a discussion. As change guru Harley Lovegrove notes, "agreeing with someone is much less hassle than rejecting their idea head on" (63).

To involve all people in finding new and better ways, a leader needs to **ensure all voices are heard**, not just the loudest ones. How:

- Actively seek ways to involve everyone in an active process to seek out different views
- Ask each member to contribute separately, even if it means in writing beforehand
- Specifically, direct questions at quieter team members to avoid loss of the lonely genius, though being sensitive to more shy group members, such as the DISC "greens"
- Ask for expert inputs to collect facts not unsubstantiated opinions
- Give people time to formulate ideas
- Ignore convention and boundaries when gathering other insights and perspectives
- Be seen to be open to contributions from all sides by listening and integrating points
- Challenge given statements and norms to question the status quo
- Seek options and alternative solutions, not problems or limitations
- Never state your viewpoint first as this will always limit new ideas from surfacing as some people are often reluctant to contradict the leader

UNDERSTANDING THE DIFFERENCE IN COMMUNICATION STYLES TO INCREASE TEAM PERFORMANCE

When we explored one-to-one communication in the previous chapters, we highlighted the importance of adapting to individuals and we introduced the DISC methodology as a useful tool as it challenges us to go beyond our natural tendencies and consider the needs of others to aid communication effectiveness or reduce friction. For leaders in groups settings, again the concept of interpersonal adaptability is paramount for influencing others and for success in different situations (64). It is important that leaders are conscious of how they work with others and be situationally appropriate, such as how to behave during presentations, meetings, interviews or meeting people for the first time.

Review the following communication styles and consider when each is most appropriate:

Decisive	Flexible	Hierarchic	Integrative
Using little information and determining one solution, communicated concisely and directly	Using little information and generating multiple solutions through informal and inclusive conversations	Using detailed information and determining one solution, communicated logically and definitively	Using detailed information and generating multiple solutions via collaborative and open dialogue with others

So, when to use each approach when working with others? Interestingly, the more senior you are, the more you need to be able to use all four approaches and know when to switch between them (64).

Decisive – This style can be associated with straight facts, practical communication, to-the-point and clear delegation. It can work when situations are not complex and when high clarity is required as it is all about tasks, actions and efficiency. In other words, good for a crisis however very poor for empathetic listening or collaboration.

Flexible – This style can appear more casual, social, even humorous, and more about adapting quickly. It is associated with more listening and expressing opinions with tact, so better where there is more complexity to consider, information needs to keep flowing and agility is key. It can however appear to short-term and discussions may appear vague. Behaviours suggest an active interest in others' ideas, points of view, and preferences, important to keep conflict at a minimum.

Hierarchic – This style of communication relies on expertise and is based upon the development and presentation of a plan. Though the plan may be structured and logical, if it was not created collaboratively, buy-in will not be achieved and the communication can appear controlling. It can however be suitable in situations where the goal is optimizing systems or processes for example as it is more about setting expectation and tasks, than genuinely influencing people.

Integrative – This style is the most suited to supporting cooperative teamwork and collaboration. It requires empathetic listening, promotes understanding and shows interest in others' ideas. It can however be slower due to high participation, multiple inputs, tolerance to differences and varied solutions being considered. It is however good for broader strategic work, creativity and exploring new ideas, concepts and outcomes. It is also more effective where the issues at hand are ambiguous, unusual, and likely to affect many people. Behaviours include actively encouraging others to share ideas and information and facilitating highly collaborative discussions that produce widely accepted decisions.

Each style type has strengths and weaknesses as seen here, however key is having the ability to consciously adopt the best style for a situation. The good news is that it is possible to develop these styles and this is necessary. Though supervisors benefit from a clear and directive communication as seen with the decisive style, at management levels, significant change must occur, and senior leaders must develop more interactive and inclusive communications. This means more openness and adapting to people and the environment around. It emphasises preference to solicit input from many people, showing interest in others' ideas and an ability to keep information flowing. The profile of use by successful senior leaders therefore indicates the **integrative is the most commonly used**, followed by flexible, then hierarchic, and decisive is least used.

I define connection as the energy that exists between people when they feel seen, heard and valued...

Brené Brown (65)

HOW NOT TO POSITIVELY STIMULATE GROUP INTERACTIONS

As a leader, balance is always required in group settings: Too little involvement can be inefficient and too much direction stifles the creativity of others.

Lack of involvement	Balanced engagement	Taking over
Issues • Can appear arrogant or disinterested (unsettling for others) • Let meetings run over time with no outcomes (inefficient)	**Personal role** • To guide towards outcome (ask questions) • To provide own expertise (share knowledge or skills) • To facilitate (provide framework or structure)	**Issues** • "My way" (demotivating for others) • No new ideas (limits innovation) • No collective problem solving (no buy-in)

In group settings, great communication is all about the mindset to collaborate, the willingness to speak up, get involved and actively contributing throughout the entire work process, but often in different personal roles.

Guiding meetings is seeking active participation to engage and include all the group, including quieter members by actively asking for their opinion, asking specific questions, summarizing points, following up on inputs and enabling the group to reach outcomes such as decisions or actions plans.

Contributing content in meetings seeks to influence the group based on valuable input such as expertise and requires clear messages that are accepted by the group. To be listened to, it is about a message that inspires others, based on a shared vision or showing what's in it for them, and using language all will understand. It is essential to explain reasoning or thinking to get buy-in and checking that others are in agreement, never assume!

Structuring meetings or **facilitating meetings** can be advantageous to manage a larger group meeting to ensure that the objectives are met effectively, with good participation and buy-in from everyone who is involved. Taking such a formal approach works when you are objective, so not necessarily involved in the topic, and key is enabling the meeting to flow from group ideas, to solutions, through to decisions. Structure can include:

- Setting the scene – welcoming, introducing people, breaking the ice, reviewing objectives and reviewing the agenda
- Controlling flow – following a model to distil data to knowledge, wisdom and outcomes
- Blending participation – balancing inputs from set speaker time to discussion time or use of breakout groups and exercises. Using questioning to augment ideas and include everyone
- Reviewing inputs, reframing, and summarizing
- Pausing and reflecting – giving individual thinking time and not coercing others
- Closing – documenting decisions, tasks and next steps

> *The nice thing about teamwork is that you always have others on your side.*
>
> Margaret Carty (66)

MINDSET WISDOM

Great communicators are generous

Generosity is the virtue of being liberal in giving of your time, information, expertise, care...

- Time is essential for relationship building
- Sharing information, not limiting or controlling access, builds transparency and trust
- Imparting expertise as a coach or mentor aids the development and progression of others
- Showing care and compassion sets in motion human exchanges that create rapport and closeness

HOW TO ACHIEVE OPTIMAL OUTCOME IN FORMAL GROUP COMMUNICATION BY PROPER PLANNING

As with one-to-one communication, group effectiveness also requires planning and often more so, due to broader audiences, less direct influence or more distant relationships, and often the need for use of more formats or tools for sharing information or materials, and allowing for asynchronous interactions.

Tips on 5 key aspects of great communication:

1. Imparting an inspiring shared vision with others so they understand why they are there, why they should listen or what's in it for them (why)
2. Creating audience-centric content / messages, using language all understand (relevant)
3. Combining different methods and tools for delivery such as mixing presentations, white board use, documents, digital tools, data, graphs, images (memorable)
4. Allowing for multi-directional, formal and informal settings to create dialogue (interactive)
5. Including positive and negative information, especially when communicating complex topics or change (believable)

Looking at suitable models for group settings, **DISC for adaptable communication** is still applicable (33). Leaders especially need to adapt to different circumstances and to modify behaviour to accommodate other ways of doing things or of relating to more people. Noticing when to modify your way can increase effectiveness. Considering the DISC methodology can be a reminder to plan for more elements of communication for all four styles or colours. This can include a good introduction or executive summary of likely results for reds; named references for yellows to understand who else is involved or who cares; data and written details for blues to analyze; more open questions and engagement for greens to get involved. A point to also remember is presence and body language. Reflect on how you may be perceived and adopt a suitable demeanour for the group setting. This could be toning down dominance or stepping up, owning more space and creating more presence through appearance and stance.

A second model we reviewed in chapter 3 was the **TALK model, for structured and impactful messages** (36). This can also be used to plan a meaningful and relevant message for a group setting:

- Being clear on the facts – what information or message needs to be conveyed
- Expressing your feelings on the situation
- Appeal to the group by giving inputs, ideas or direction
- Frame your relationship with the group to leverage team spirit

TRYING TO INSPIRE?

Communication is so much more than facts. Let's look at an example of what happens when only facts are in focus:

Maria sent out an email to a newly formed project team. She had carefully created a project plan with sub-projects, assigned tasks and deadlines all listed. She also included updated process information to ensure all were clear on expected methodologies and reporting tools.

Maria was surprised to receive many questions, followed by demands for meetings from people not happy to be allocated work in this manner.

The issue?

Skill – Though useful as a project to-do-list, such a communication is not going to win the hearts of the project team as it focuses only on what to do, by whom and by when. Jumping to methodologies also may come across as controlling the way people must work.

It is not inspiring to just receive instructions on your tasks and deadlines in such a directive way.

How to do better:

Even a project plan can share more inspiring material:
- Project purpose – why this project is so important
- Scope and success factors – a framework and focus for results / outcomes
- Stakeholders – understanding the complexity of those with an interest in the success of the project and whose needs must be factored in and communicated with
- Milestones – reference points for key reviews, checks, major deliverables, major events or decisions
- Key Actions / Steps – structure and main project aspects to show a complete picture
- Resources – transparency on team and tools
- Risks – honesty on known issues that require attention or caution

The quality of information conveyed, including the timeliness, accuracy and perceived usefulness are important determinants of employee reactions (7), however receivers also have emotional reactions to messages, such as why should I care, who is asking and what is being asked of me? Great communication goes beyond facts to connect with people and consider these emotional aspects.

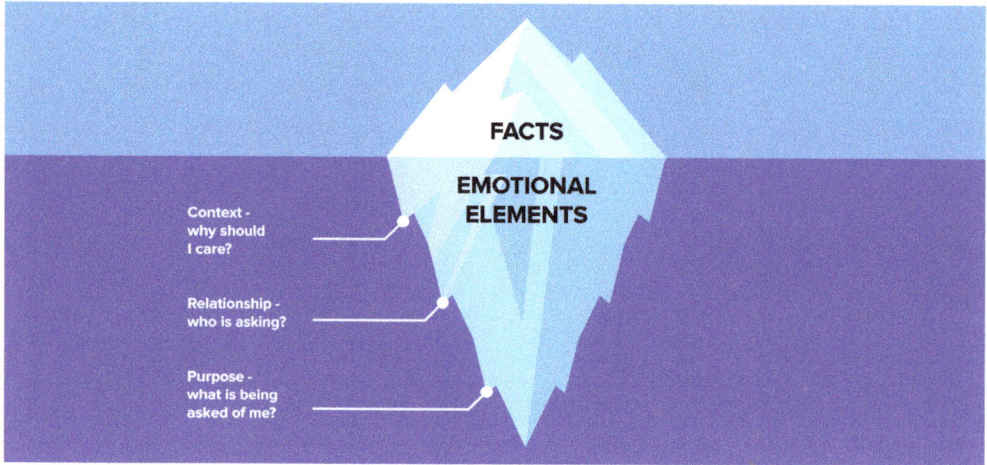

Figure 13: Message content must include factual and emotional aspects

The daily challenge is that most work communication is factual, detailed and operational, focused on what to do, how to do, who does it by when etc. Though important, this is not the inspiring part or the part that links to emotions. For example, to grab attention and engage others, is all about audience-relevant messages that are simple and short, and in the order people want to listen to.

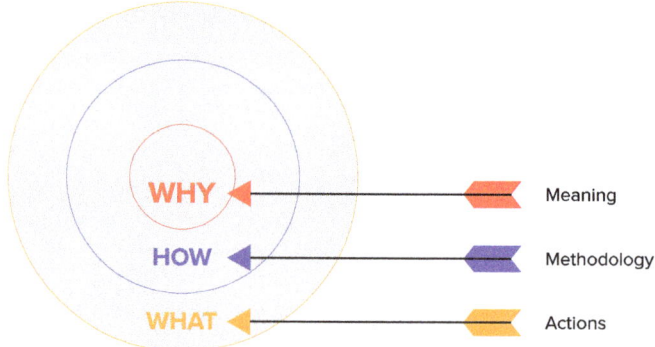

Figure 14: Starting with why (67)

To engage people on a more emotional level, the message must explain the **WHY first**, the part that is core and deeper — the underwater part of the iceberg. There are two forces that govern human behaviour, why and how. Why is the motive for doing something, the meaning. **HOW** is the method of doing it, the part that is objective and detailed. When it comes to engagement and buy-in, motive trumps method, in other words, why trumps how. Easier said than done though as how and what (actions) are simpler and less stressful to talk about in many situations.

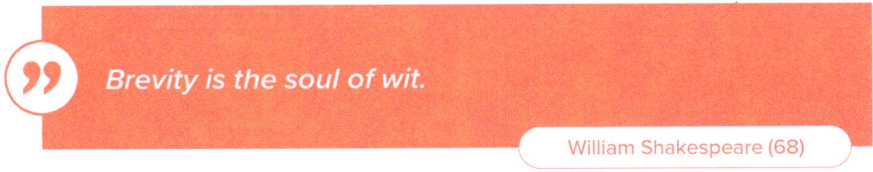

> *Brevity is the soul of wit.*
>
> William Shakespeare (68)

BREVITY WITH BRIEF

A great way to **craft an inspiring and memorable message is to use the BRIEF methodology** (69). David McCormack developed BRIEF as a guideline to communicate complex topics in a clear, focused, and compelling way. In his book "Brief: Make a bigger impact by saying less", the full technique is explained, and we will summarize it here as it is a useful tool for leaders. It targets attracting and maintaining attention and getting your point across. Emphasis is placed on short and simple messages to avoid distraction due to limited attention spans.

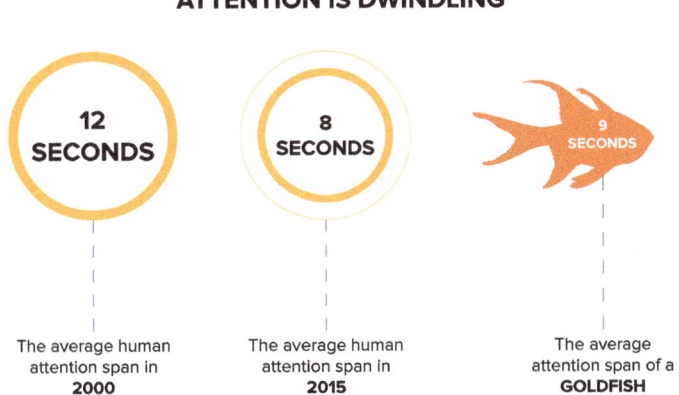

Figure 15: The problem with attention span (69)

The starting point is the **headline** to grab attention through content, intrigue and to the point. For example, think about how you use the subject line in emails. If the subject is vague, the entire email needs to be read, or it is simply deleted. If the core information is in the subject line, it is immediately clear what it is all about. The second step, the **"narrative map"** is used to build a clearly structured, concise and compelling story, memorable to refocus attention every 8 seconds. This covers the "why", the context and the best flow of information for others to follow.

Part 1: The Real-Life Work Situations (and Models to Help)

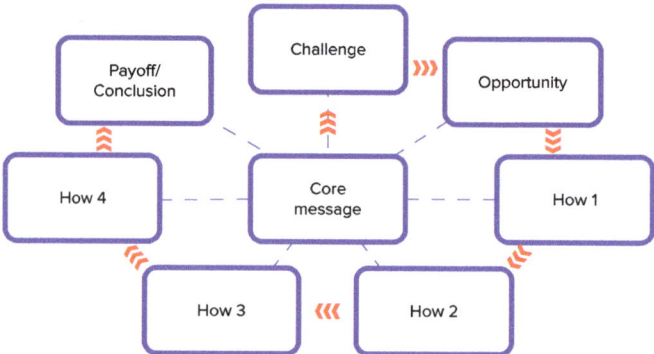

Figure 16: The BRIEF narrative map (69)

The figure shows a schematic representation of the narrative map as a basic structure for the transfer of information, for example in a presentation. The map works clockwise. It starts with the development of the core message.

Core message - This can be compared to a headline that illustrates the core of the story, what the story is about, and why it´s important. The core message needs to be short and spark the audience's interest.

Challenge - This field allows you to describe which problem, conflict or challenge exists, in one or two sentences. In other words, summarizing why or how the problem exists.

Opportunity - This field offers the "aha" moment. It is constructed according to the "what if" principle: What if we could find a different or better option? The point is to show what the possibilities are, what is the unfulfilled need that will be fulfilled. It describes what may solve the problem.

How 1-4 are considered to be supporting statements - In these fields, the specifics or steps of implementation are described, key topic areas or what the process is to achieve the fix. Key here is to focus on the essential information to avoid getting lost in detail.

Payoff / Conclusion - A good story people will remember needs a catchy end. It's about showing what the end result is - the ultimate success – and this needs to stick in peoples' minds. It needs to describe what ultimate success looks like.

The narrative map is a good way to prepare messages and structure your thoughts in a systematic visualization of core ideas. By jotting down statements in this logical way it helps reduce complexity and achieve concise, inspirational content.

To help you understand what this looks like in practise, as an example, we will share the map we created when we started working on this book. You can see the sections with concise text and from our scribbled notes, how this relates to the models and chapters of the book.

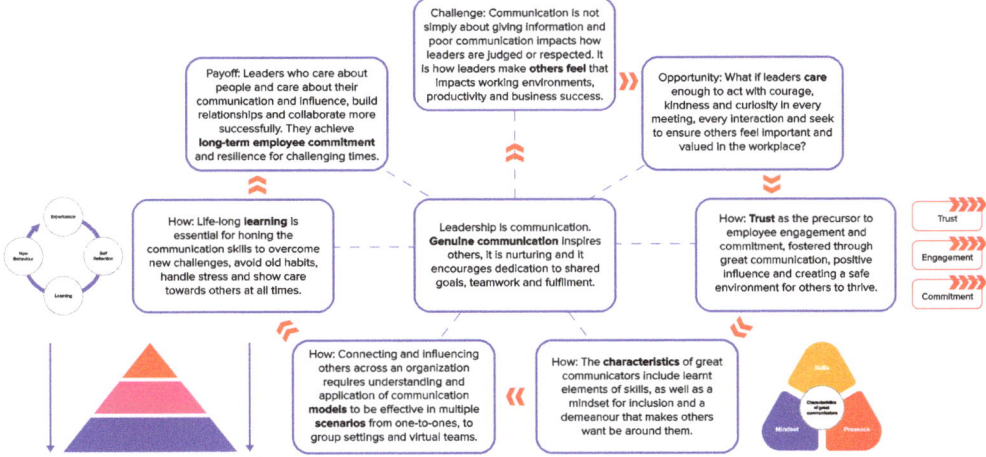

Figure 17: Example of a BRIEF map for "Connecting and Influencing: A leader's guide to genuine communication"

WHAT IF YOUR AUDIENCE ARE SENIOR EXECS?

Do you need to consider anything else? Many people say that they struggle to influence the senior executives in their organization. There are several reasons for this gap:

- Failure to understand senior executive / C-suite needs
- Failure to handle lack of feedback
- Failure to handle unexpected changes in meetings
- Missing some element of skill, mindset or presence development to stay focused and on message

Firstly, think about what senior leaders care about. Their job is **strategic and future-focused**, meaning they are absorbed in anticipating and planning for years ahead, not the day-to-day. This means that they want to hear about the world outside, the customer perspective, competitor perspectives, industry trends, best practices, technological innovations, economics etc. In other words, inputs that challenge the status quo, may drive efficiency or effectiveness, give competitive advantage or set out a new opportunity or direction for the business. Never big them down in your tasks, as that is your job.

Secondly, when invited to a meeting with senior leaders, it will be based on your expertise, experience or reputation. It is therefore expected that you will share insights and do it well. Again, it is your job, so never anticipate overwhelming praise for doing this. Remember great communication needs high emotional intelligence and this includes **self-motivation not external recognition**.

Thirdly, senior leaders will be time poor and often distractable. Despite best efforts, leadership meetings tend not to follow agendas and timelines very strictly. This can lead to allotted presentation times being cut from 1 hour to 10 minutes on the spot. It happens! It means anyone preparing to present needs a backup plan and the "**executive summary**". Preparing messages following the BRIEF concept helps ensure you can stay focused and on message under pressure.

In summary, what is your clear story, plan, timeline and value for company or customer? What is your goal in the meeting? Is it to sell an idea or position your team? Is it to inspire? Is it to achieve a fast decision or project sign off? In terms of structure and content, have a simple and clear take-home message, provide all key information and aim for a good customer-centric story. Make sure the financials are accurate, present a proposed solution (never a problem), and show timelines for implementation. In terms of delivery, show your knowledge and conviction with a believable message. Focus on customer or company value and balance facts with emotional wins. And remember to keep smiling even if you only get 5 minutes to share your inputs!

THE CHALLENGES OF VIRTUAL COMMUNICATION

Communication and collaboration are often easier with people in the same office, yet with the rise of team members in remote or home locations, leaders need to reconsider communication and collaboration for virtual scenarios. The challenge comes from **distance** impacting all relationships: leader influence reduces, employee self-responsibility increases, and colleague social aspects suffer. The result can be disconnection from the business, loss of motivation, reduced productivity, isolation and fatigue.

So how to build and maintain long term relations, despite distance? Not only is this about having the tools and technologies for regular communication and collaboration, it is also about trust, two-way mutual trust. This starts with truth, the ability to admit failures or discuss misunderstandings. It's also doing what you say, taking time to explain when others need to know more. It's creating positive team spirit and it requires the willingness to work with others, complete tasks together, and share knowledge, information, learnings etc across the team. The intent of establishing and maintaining a good working atmosphere needs to start with leaders and yes, extra efforts are required when the team is far apart and can't simply go for coffee or have a beer after work.

To overcome the specific challenges of virtual collaboration, the solutions are multifactorial, both physical, related to the environment, access to the business and use of technology, and emotional, related to the connections you make around you.

The physical is not considered here, but it is about getting organized, allocating workspace and establishing new routines. **Access to the business** is worth mentioning as it is the remit of a leader to ensure that remote workers have access to everything they need to do their job and be effective. This includes constant access to work content so they can work when they want and how they want. It is removing barriers and ensuring employees are not frustrated by technology issues that may hinder productivity. To ensure this, the technology and tools for virtual collaboration must work well! Employees also need to be well trained on the systems and have easy access to the business information they need.

During lockdown, Angela was struggling to get updates on projects from one of her team members. Even in team meetings, this employee was vague on delivery dates. Sending emails with specific questions also failed to elicit the necessary information.

The issue?

Mindset – Leading virtual workers puts more demands on leaders. However, it is the leader's responsibility to ensure people can succeed! Leaders need to spend more time reaching out to employees and need to show more care towards the feelings and wellbeing of potentially isolated workers.

How to do better:

Connecting with remote workers:
- Establish more frequent one-to-ones - even if they are short, it is better to have more regular contact
- Pick up the phone or use video as much as possible to connect with people, rather than rely on digital media – reach out!
- Never assume remote workers will come to you with issues – especially when people are un-used to remote working, it is better to check-in with them on work and non-work topics
- Do not fall into the trap of over-controlling when work is not visible – focus on results and trust more

HOW TO BUILD TEAM RELATIONSHIPS EVEN IN THE VIRTUAL WORLD?

The **emotional challenge of distance is all about staying connected to people**, and it includes social elements. The bond and togetherness from "water cooler chat" is possible in the virtual business world. The 2 billion Facebook users is testament to the social abilities of humans to connect across the world when there is shared interest to do so! Rituals also matter. Spirit and culture come from rituals and it is possible to use technology and tools to establish new rituals for the virtual team. These can be as simple as how meetings are opened, how chat apps are used or even having crazy virtual backgrounds... co-created rituals have even more power. Finally, it is still all about team building that comes from the social not only the work interactions. Do things together as a virtual team – huddles, shared coffee breaks and even after work beers are surprisingly nice when done via video chat.

Though sophisticated tools are required for more effective virtual communication, the team **performance depends on how people use these technologies**, not on the technologies themselves, though these should be matched to the task or goal (55). For effective virtual collaboration there needs to be a mix of tools and users need the ability to use them. Available options should include tools or apps for formal meetings, such as zoom. Informal channels should be encouraged for social or quick chat, such as whatsapp or slack. Systematic file sharing and document storage must also be planned, as well as formal collaborative project management systems, for example trello. These formal systems need policies, access rights, long term storage and updating options.

Other best practices are linked to the **mindset for inclusive communication and collaboration**:

- Make intentions clear – review messages before sending them to make sure the right tone is struck
- Stay in sync - prioritize keeping everyone in the loop, maintain regular communication with team members, and avoid lengthy silences
- Be responsive, supportive, open and inclusive
- Take more active steps to overcome group phenomena – create a safe environment in which others are willing to speak up and ensure all voices are heard through integrative dialogue

CAREFULLY CHOOSING THE BEST VIRTUAL TOOL IS ESSENTIAL

As a footnote, **virtual communication and collaboration tools** differ along a number of dimensions, including information richness and the level of real-time interaction that is possible. The purpose of the communication should determine the delivery mechanism:

Asynchronous and text-based media such as email, chat, and bulletin boards work well for pushing information in one direction, circulating routine information and plans. For resolving interpersonal issues, email or chat should be avoided and synchronous (live) and richer media used instead.

Other asynchronous tools include **digital formats for file sharing and project management** allowing for exchange of information without the requirement for all the recipients to respond immediately. Benefits include:

- Focus on work without being constantly interrupted
- Providing a chance to think twice—most people don't make the best decisions when they are pressured to answer on the spot
- Individuals can decide when to check and respond to communications
- A record of communication exists
- Allowing more effective communication with remote teams, especially spread across different time zones, or across the wider organization

Note, **email** is an asynchronous communication tool in theory as it allows responses later. The problem with email is that most people use it as a synchronous tool. Leaders often expect employees to answer emails as if they were picking up the phone. As a result, employees waste considerable time answering emails in real-time, not in line with the principles of asynchronous communication.

Web-based audio conferencing and video conferencing are more interactive tools better suited to complex tasks and issues such as problem-solving, seeking different ideas and perspectives. These give the live and lively interactions great for team participation and real collaboration.

Overall, the more complex the task, the closer people should be to in-person communication, and sometimes meeting face-to-face is the best option.

Examples of actions to connect and influence others despite distance:		
Ensure access	Build relationships	Maintain motivation
• Provide technology and tools needed for productivity • Role model use of tools • Be available for people • Be helpful on how / where to find information	• Increase one-to-one frequency and use video as much as possible • Use team meetings for updates, sharing information and group work • Establish regular team social time such as a weekly coffee session to talk non-work • Use informal chats to reach out and ask how people are • Remember active inclusion of all members	• Reiterate vision and shared goals more often • Share information more generously • Be a role model for openness and inclusiveness • Acknowledge people • Show appreciation • Get to know individuals better
Trust, time and technology are the secrets of virtual communication and collaboration!		

"Coming together is a beginning. Keeping together is progress. Working together is success."

Henry Ford (70)

Summary of Connecting and Influencing in Groups

Concept Level	Audience scenario	Goal	Communication Characteristics			Models	Additional virtual considerations
			Skills	Mindset	Presence		
Collaboration	Team & group settings	Participation, inclusion & inspiration	- Sharing ideas & information - Running effective meetings - Overcoming groupthink - Integrating others - Facilitating - Planning concise communications - Mixing the synchronous and asynchronous	- Trust - Showing care - Including everyone - Generosity	- Positive body language - Giving attention - Investing time	- DISC - TALK - Group styles - Balanced engagement - WHY - BRIEF - Connecting despite distance	- Live(ly) interactions - Use of technology

Chapter 5:

LET'S PUT IT IN WRITING

Key knowledge

- To extend communication and influence more broadly requires more care as what is put in writing must avoid any possible misinterpretations, as it often has a long shelf life
- For broader communication, multiple tools need to be deployed for impactful messages and to allow for response elements
- Beyond skills to create content, digital and media skills are also required for effective online presence

Key models

- Tools for 2-way reach
- AIDA for content flow
- Range versus depth model
- Online influence
- Networking dimensions

Impact

- Broader reach within an organization and beyond, can create strong identity and a network for expanding knowledge

In this chapter we consider the bottom layer of our model (see figure 18), where we seek influence of wider audiences such as reach across an organization, and beyond. Again, the challenges become greater as direct influence is removed when try to connect with many more people, such a global teams and networks. The format of communication also becomes much more asynchronous, where messages are often confined to writing or the online world.

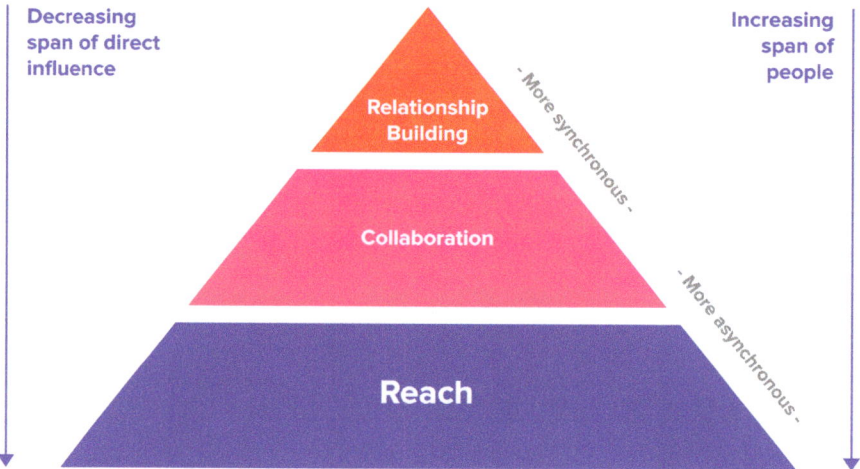

Figure 18: Ability to communicate and maintain influence at all levels is required in business

As George Bernard Shaw (27) said, "the single biggest problem in communication is the illusion that it has taken place". This is even more true for asynchronous communication to large audiences, as pressing "send" on an email is not communication! So, let's explore how to keep in touch well.

Especially with the virtual scenario in mind, the aim of communication must extend from simply throwing out information, to considering goals, open access, as well as timeliness of information sharing and making broader communication not simply one-directional but two-directional, meaning response elements are included.

After a recent meeting, Alex decided more action was required to ensure follow up on the group tasks. He sent four emails in quick succession to remind or update team members of what to do and by when. He was careful to only include relevant people in each email and he remembered to keep each email short.

1. To project managers: Attached pdf is the project plan file for you to share...
2. To the analytics team: All data is in the shared folder, section headed March...
3. To the content experts: Next milestone is in 10 days, so get your reports to your project managers by 5pm the day before...
4. To the stakeholders in senior management: All on track...

The issue?

Skill – Not only should communication be inspiring and memorable; it should also be relevant and interactive as much as possible. In this example, relevance could have been improved by making it as easy as possible for the recipients:

- Sending a pdf makes use of documents much more difficult
- For ease of access, hyperlinks are ideal routes to file locations and better than trying to describe where to go
- Always consider standard formats for reports etc – if there is one, attached the template
- When keeping stakeholders up to date, a reminder of the goal and the specifics of the status is a better memory boost, as well as being more believable. Vagueness never sounds convincing!

How to do better:

Key questions to always consider:

- What outcome do you want to achieve?
- Have you provided all information the other people need to act or make a decision for example?
- Could you simplify or tweak the communication to make it easier to understand?

HOW TO MAKE BROADER COMMUNICATION INTERACTIVE

For two-way reach that includes response elements the more synchronous (live) the communication the better, yet the focus on digital formats for reach tends to add more asynchronous tools. What's important to remember is that one-way communication only pushes information, but it does not create dialogue, enable collaboration or build new ideas. Two-way communication, even to broad audiences is still about building relationships. So how to achieve the richness of communication needed?

Firstly, **WHY** do you want to reach a broad audience – do you have something unique to say or expertise to share to joint projects?

Be specific on **WHO** you want to reach to define what language / languages to use. You may need to modify language to accommodate a potentially less advanced vocabulary. If you really want to reach out, make it simple for others to want to join in.

Thirdly, **WHAT** you say is not just the vocabulary in written or spoken forms, but also the punctuation can alter the message. Tone of voice is also critical in live interactions.

Choosing **WHERE** to communicate or what tools to use is then the key part for 2-way reach. **HOW** can others engage or respond? Have you thought through how you follow up on responses?

Finally, think about **WHEN** you deliver your message. Although interaction may be the aim, the benefit of much virtual communication is that the response does not have to be immediate. It must be considered that recipients may not see the message immediately or choose to reflect before responding. The type of message may also impact when and how it is shared, for example, it's not a great idea to leave bad news in someone's inbox to be the first thing they read after they wake up. Also, take time when designing virtual communications. With a wide reach and longevity of media, the impact of a message, good or bad, could last a very long time.

DIFFERENT TOOLS FOR DIFFERENT PURPOSES

Whichever tool is used for reach, it is usually combined with others to balance reach, depth of content and interaction. Key is being consistent with use and message.

- **Chat tools** are just that; informal and great for making up for lack of face-to-face contact. However, as much as people may love to chat on Slack, if the discussion becomes too confusing or complex, you need to switch to detail-enabled written formats, or even phone or video calls.
- **Emails** are often the simplest way to communicate with known contacts, especially professionally, however, younger workforce entrants for example, don't use email regularly.
- Many **project management tools** work well to collate and store all task- and project-related materials and conversations, however access is controlled.
- **Online discussion forum** allow interaction between many people, location and time independent. They can be internal or external. Options include joining established groups or setting up new ones, however, strict management of content and participation, to guide and stimulate meaningful conversation is essential. Online, participants have flexibility and control over the time they spend on any topic, it can allow anonymous participation to encourage reluctant members to share their viewpoint and it allows participants to contribute and communicate simultaneously on different topics. However, due to this time constraint, there is a delay between the message exchange which can lead to loss of interest and affects the contextual structure and coherence of the discussion. The participation also needs to be understood and managed for better interactions (71, 72, 73. 74, 75, 76, 77).

In general, in group settings, conformity is seen as a positive group behaviour as it drives socially acceptable behaviour including following rules and politeness. However, within any team questionable behaviour can also be seen, as discussed in group phenomena. Issues specific to virtual teams are the "lurker participants" and "flaming participants" that can occur with anonymity.

Lurkers are also known as the silent group. These are people who do not participate publicly. Why? Reasons include:

- They feel there is no need – for them just reading the available information is enough
- They need to connect with the whole group before they will join in
- They don't believe they are helping when others have already made their point, or they have no input or expertise
- They can't get the technology to work
- They don't actually like the group dynamics

For such situations, the more active the online community the better, yet it also requires the community owner to seek inputs, send please join messages, even use direct emails to encourage participation. Especially for lurkers, a general rule of introducing people in virtual environments and facilitating team building is required to connect people first.

Flaming on the other hand relates to written e-communications, where virtual spaces allow people to write things they would seldom say face-to-face. Comments are generally considered to be hostile and insulting. The reasoning is often psychologically complex, including entertainment, passing time or aggression. It is also more commonly seen from men. Flaming does cause emotional distress and has been suggested to reduce productivity in the workplace and contribute to loss of business. As part of ethical behaviour, communication policies, cyber security and risk management programs, organizations should take proactive steps to prevent or reduce flaming in any electronic communication. The goal of virtual collaboration must be safe participation for all.

MINDSET WISDOM

Great communicators understand reaching out

Mass communication is not limited to the "marketing department". The mindset to reach others as a leader includes goals to:

- Communicate content – effectively sharing as well as understanding information flow
- Establish and maintain relationships - creating and understanding relationship messages and engaging others
- Build and maintain identity – articulating personal experiences, self-representation and establishing self-image

WHAT TO CONSIDER WHEN CREATING "MASS" COMMUNICATION

Setting out to write something down for broad communication can be daunting without proper consideration. It's not just the skills to write an effective message, it also requires digital and media skills.

1. Content creation needs logical structure

As we looked at with BRIEF (69), flow of information is important. To grab attention, it is all about taking in headlines, audience-relevant messages that are simple and short and in the order people listen to. To engage people on a more emotional level, the message must explain the "why" first and the context, so that a topic actually means something to them. Only then are they motivated to act accordingly. Another useful model to apply for written formats is AIDA (78).

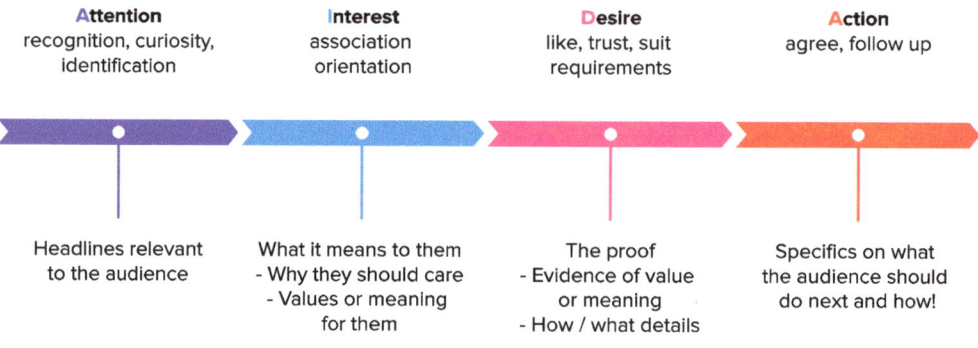

Figure 19: The AIDA model for written flow

In this model, the stages are: Headlines to get attention, meaning to gain interest (the why), evidence or proof to create desire (the what / how) and actions clearly defined to explain the next steps. This model was developed for creating marketing messages, yet the principles are the same and can be applied to communicating to employees.

Imagine the email scenario again. When the subject header is not clear or the main points are lost in detailed paragraphs or the data files or links are not included or the next steps are not specific, the email is pointless! It is likely to be ignore or deleted. It is just as frustrating as an email blast from your favourite shop which includes a picture of a new item you desperately want to buy and yet there is no buying information included... Make it as simple as possible for people to do business with you. Make it as simple as possible for colleagues to interact with you.

2. Reach requires basic digital abilities

With the rate of change in society and business driving more digital communication and virtual collaboration, digital competence is required by everyone. This means the ability to find, evaluate and contribute information using digital platforms. The European Union describes digital competence as a "set of knowledge, skills and attitudes ... that are required when using information communication technology and digital media" (79) and these skills and knowledge refer to abilities associated with data literacy, communication, collaboration, as well as content creation, safety and technical problem solving (80).

Technology really is the norm and a digital mind set is a new leadership competency (81, 82). Leaders need knowledge of digital system technologies and skills to be proficient in the use of technology. A digital mind set sees and actively makes use of the opportunities coming with new technologies. It is not all about the technology per se, it means enabling information flow, leveraging online communication tools, using technology to make communication easier with distant teams and networks.

3. Reach requires media savviness

Media competencies are the knowledge, skills and strategies that allow an individual to efficiently handle mass communication. What is important today with the expansion of technology and social media is going beyond simply consuming information, to learning how to contribute it to. Media literacy is the ability to actively use all kinds of media for communication (83). There are many dimensions to media competence (83, 84, 85), yet key for leaders are the following:

- Cognitive dimension – the knowledge, understanding and ability to analyze or critically review media content and tools
- Design dimension – related to the skills of content design itself
- Action dimension – the usage of media tools from designing, expressing and informing. In other words, of not only consuming media, but actively shaping it oneself.

Once the content is defined, to get the message through to the right audience, the right media must be used for mass communication. This mean defining the formats or channels such as online platforms, email, websites etc and the set plans in place to implement. In today's world, the options for where to communicate are immense and leaders need to define the most appropriate channels and tools based on the goal of the communication. Media skills can develop more effectiveness in creating the content for sharing or publishing, especially on external platforms, such as Linkedin.

One view is to consider the target audience. For internal messaging, both online and offline options exist depending upon content and reach. For external audiences, choices can be specific for mass communication or more targeted to networks and can also include online and offline tools.

Part 1: The Real-Life Work Situations (and Models to Help)

	Internal	External
Online	Emails Chats Intranet …	Company web Social media Blogs, Twitter …
Offline	Meetings Printed materials …	Seminars Printed materials …

Figure 20: Tools for broader communication

A good example of when reach is required across an organization is during significant organizational change. The degree to which employees embrace organizational changes is largely dependent on their trust in leaders and this trust depends to a large degree on whether the employees have received adequate information about the changes and the reasons for them (7). In such an instance, the quality of information, timeliness, accuracy, depth, frequency and usefulness all play an important determinant of reactions. To cover such complexity, different forms of communication must be mixed, so synchronous and asynchronous. All media types and channels should also be mixed. It is always essential to therefore plan broader communication, determine all tools to engage a wider group and mix tools and technologies to provide information and stimulate two-way dialogue. Specifically, in the change scenario, tools can be differentiated by range, so how many employees can be reached, and depth of impact, the level of change possible as a response to the tool (86). In such a scenario, a combination of verbal and written tools is recommended to transfer multiple messages and to reinforce messages over time.

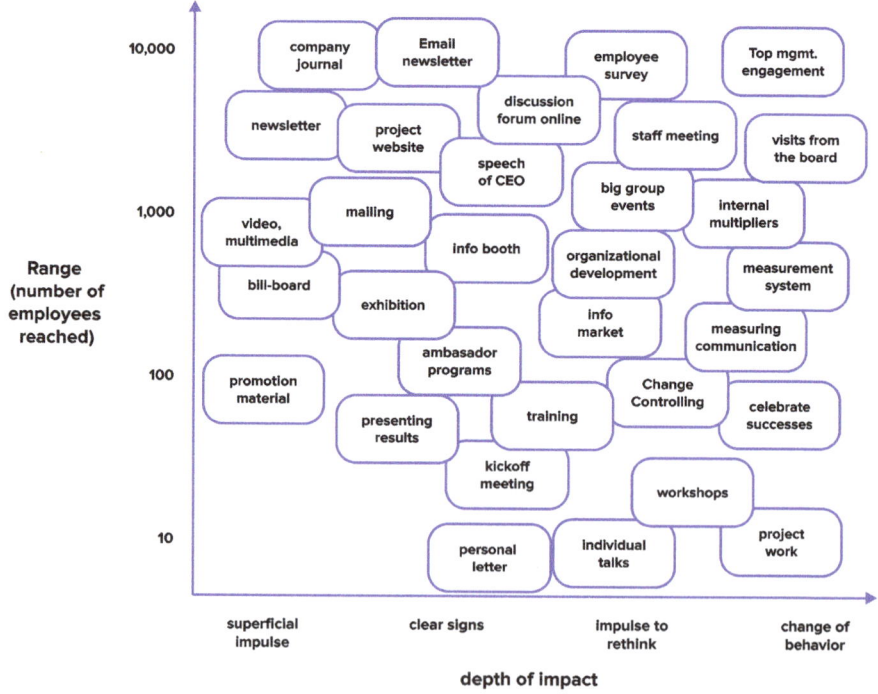

Figure 21: Range / depth model for communicating change

The primary goal however of media competencies and related communication is to communicate content, establish and maintain social relationships, and to build and maintain identity. For a deeper dive into how to develop content, see chapter 7.

BUSINESS USE OF SOCIAL MEDIA

Do you use social media? Is your use personal or business or both? Social media is any digital tool that allows users to quickly create and share content and facilitates sharing of information, ideas, career interests and other forms of expression via virtual communities and networks.

Having received a fifth advert message in a week, Stefan logged on to his LinkedIn account. He did not use the site much but felt his name should be listed at least. When he looked at it, he was not sure the old goofy T-shirt picture, numerous likes of silly stories, list of hobbies and outdated information really did give the best impression.

The issue?

Skill – Skill – Writing and posting online content requires planning and care as digital material has a long shelf-life and global reach.

Presence – Image is everything!

How to do better:

Skills for building positive external reach:
- Set goals and consider why post?
- What valuable information or expertise do you have to share?
- Are images or shared stories business appropriate?
- Can you upload material that looks effective, with working links etc?
- How often do you update your information or check for responses?
- Who can see your posts?
- Do you send the image you really wish to convey?

Embracing social media isn't just a bit of fun, it's a vital way to communicate, keep your ear to the ground and improve your business.

Richard Branson (87)

Whatever your opinion is of social media, be sure to know that it is here to stay! The first recognizable social media site, Six Degrees, was created in 1997. It enabled users to upload a profile and make friends with other users. In 1999, the first blogging sites became popular, creating a social media sensation that's still popular today. Sites like MySpace and LinkedIn gained prominence in the early 2000s, and sites like Photobucket and Flickr facilitated online photo sharing. YouTube came out in 2005, creating an entirely new way for people to communicate and share with each other across great distances. By 2006, Facebook and Twitter both became available to users throughout the world. These sites remain some of the most popular social networks on the Internet (88).

Here are some key social media statistics for 2020 (89), that are relevant for businesses:

- 3.5 billion social media users worldwide (and that's 45% of the world's population). >90% of Millennials, 77% of Generation X, and 48% of Baby Boomers are active users
- Facebook is the most popular social media
- Users spend an average of 3 hours per day on social networks and messaging.
- 73% of marketers believe that social media marketing has been "somewhat effective" or "very effective" for their business
- 54% of social browsers use social media to research products
- 71% of consumers who have had a positive experience with a brand on social media are likely to recommend the brand to their friends and family
- 49% of consumers depend on influencer recommendations on social media

So, apart from the headline statistics, why else should leaders in the digital age care about the utilization of technologies for active sharing and personal presence in the online world of social media? Today, many leaders choose to produce social media content, write blogs, use twitter etc, as a new opportunity to share knowledge and experience. Such channels offer exciting and new reach to spread information.

There are many reasons why leaders should **be active and visible online** and make it a priority (90):

- To position yourself and the company as experts - people believe that executive-level engagement on social media demonstrates industry expertise and leadership
- To earn the trust of others - customers are more likely to trust a company whose leadership team are active online
- To engage with customers using social media uses more personal channels, communicating the more human side of the business
- To attract the best talent - employees believe that CEOs who engage on social media are better equipped to lead companies in the modern world
- To set a good example for employee actions - content shared by employees drives more engagement than content shared via branded corporate channels (91)
- To add wider value - one of the most enriching consequences of digital engagement is the opportunity to influence the environment better. Companies don't operate in isolation and the online world provides opportunity to support ideas, values and initiatives aligned with company goals

Influencers in social media are people who have built a reputation for their knowledge and expertise on a specific topic. They make regular posts about that topic on their preferred social media channels and generate large followings of enthusiastic, engaged people who pay close attention to their views. In other words, they influence the decision making of others.

The bulk of influencer marketing today occurs in social media from so called micro-influencers, ordinary everyday people who have become known for their knowledge about some specialist niche. Bloggers are perceived to have the most authentic and active relationships with their fans and as such, brands are now recognizing and encouraging this. Another favourite type of content is video and most create a channel on YouTube, becoming YouTubers. Podcasters are fast gaining popularity and podcasts have now become more mainstream as episodic series of spoken word digital audio files that a user can download to a personal device for easy listening.

The level of influence achievable can vary a great deal. Celebrities were the original influencers. Of interest to businesses and of more relevance to every day leaders is the influence achieved by key opinion leaders. Industry experts and thought leaders can also be considered influencers. These are people who gain respect because of their qualifications, position, or experience about their topic of expertise. Often, this respect is earned more because of the reputation of where they work.

Circling back to consider digital communication, collaboration and virtual reach, the concept of social media influencers also links to the role and value of **networking**. In this context, a more worthy goal is the use of broader media tools to share knowledge and experience. Networking can be considered the establishing of mutually beneficial relationships, influence and exchange of ideas. Online communities are a great example of virtual networking. In terms of connecting today, the internet really does have great power!

Networking is not about just connecting people. It's about connecting people with people, people with ideas, and people with opportunities.

Michele Jennae (92)

USING THE INTERNET TO BROADEN YOUR NETWORK

The internet and social media are causing our environment to be increasingly characterized by a feeling of cooperation and interconnectedness (93). For example, Facebook has changed the social life of our species and evidence shows its use to connect people with specialist interests, sharing information and experiences (94). This rise in "networking", the exchange of ideas among individuals or groups that share a common interest, will continue. In business, this exchange of information includes seeking new ideas or broader perspectives from within an organization or from outside, for knowledge enhancement. Other benefits are (95, 96, 97):

- Visibility – communicating with partners on a regular basis to maintain business relationships
- New contacts - meeting potential clients or identify opportunities for partnerships, joint ventures, or new areas of expansion for the business
- Staying current - keeping up with market conditions and overall industry trends
- Problem solving - finding solutions to business problems or needs
- Confidence and morale – a boost from spending time with optimistic and successful people
- Innovation - unique collaborations and industry networks are springing up to increase the probabilities of innovation success

Networks can be internal or external, formal or informal. Activity relies on effective communication skills and a mindset believing that networking is an important task for leaders, requiring the allocation of sufficient time and effort to see it pay off. If you are to invest time in building networks, face-to-face or digital, key considerations include deciding which networks to reach out to and what skills are required for effective networking.

WHICH NETWORKS MAKE SENSE?

To improve overall connectedness, four dimensions can be considered; the size, strength, pattern and resources available (98). Size refers to the number of members in the network. Strength of relationships, both strong and weak, are of importance. The pattern of relationships looks at connecting with people outside normal groups and expanding to other communities. Finally, the resources dimension is about determining which connections are useful and deciding which connections are beneficial to both parties.

Four networking dimensions:

Size

Having a larger friendship network is positively related to social integration, increased organizational knowledge and task mastery. Building and maintaining relationships with others results in a larger network that individuals can turn to for social support, ideas, advise or sponsorship.

Networking behaviours to help increase and maintain network size:

- Increase internal visibility, actively engaging in conversations in videoconferences & in person
- Engage in professional activities
- Participate in social gatherings and events
- Maintain contact with others by keeping in touch, such as monthly lunches & coffee

Getting started: Begin with connecting with people you know first. When connecting with people you do not yet know, start with what you may have in common.

Strength

The strength of a connection in a network can be assessed based on the frequency of contact, degree of intimacy, and emotional investment, with weak ties on one end of the continuum and strong ties on the other (99).

Both weak and strong ties can be very useful:

- Acquaintances can be more useful for finding jobs as they are a source of more unique information (close contacts tend to know about similar openings)
- Strong ties are often necessary for obtaining complex information (99). Strong relationships may be more important for the transfer of sensitive or complex information than weak ones due to the higher risk and effort involved (100).

Pattern

The pattern of relationships determines whether the members of an individual network are connected to one another. A gap in a network exists when there is no connection between two members. Most professionals build their network over time through proximity — most work in the same field or industry, people from business school or colleagues from a current company or past jobs. Most have few outliers in the mix unless deliberate about networking. Members who do not know each other are more likely to provide diverse information so try to connect with people outside of typical circles of acquaintances (101). Such reach is easily facilitated online and professional organizations and tools such as LinkedIn can be leveraged.

To diversify:

- Inventory of existing connections - think about where a network is closed and where there are opportunities to diversify
- Put networking on the schedule
- Ask for recommendations
- Be in it for the long term to fulfil personal curiosity and develop personal. Professional return is a happy coincidence

> **Resources**
>
> The resources or usefulness of a network are the benefits that can be derived from the relationships.
>
> Resources can be in the form of information and ideas, social support, job search assistance or business assistance such as providing leads or access to resources.
>
> It is not about connecting with someone specifically to gain favour; it is recognizing what resources you and others have and what resources you could share that might be useful and therefore create mutual benefit.
>
> Determining the usefulness of a relationship is about making the right connections, trying to avoid wasting someone's time and recognizing when to strengthen a relationship and when to let it remain a weak tie. To achieve this, develop a clear picture of good connections and set goals. When reaching out it is very important to have a clear reason why you want to meet a specific person. Also consider what you have to offer. This is about your personal brand.
>
> When creating your personal brand, ask yourself:
> - What are my strengths, what am I known for?
> - What am I passionate about, what sets me apart?
> - What would I like to accomplish in my life?
> - How do I define success?
> - What do I want employers or contacts to remember about me?

WHICH SKILLS DO YOU NEED FOR NETWORKING?

Whether you are reaching out in formal groups or extending a personal network, the skills for effective networking are similar to working in virtual teams and broader collaborations. It is still aimed at achieving influence, hence necessitating building trust, investing time in people and leveraging the right technology.

- For strengthening of network connections and relationships, **emotional intelligence** can be developed, governing ability to relate to people while managing own emotions and those of others (11). This is crucial for connecting with others, building trust and establishing genuine rapport. In the context of networking, the following are important:

    o **Openness to experience** counts as effective networking involves stepping out of your comfort zone. A simple solution is to say yes - attend events, accept invitations, join activities and volunteer to get involved. Individuals who are high in openness to experience are curious, broad-minded, imaginative and open to trying new techniques (102).

    o **Ambiguity tolerance** can be defined as the degree to which an individual is comfortable with uncertainty, unpredictability, conflicting directions and multiple demands. A tolerance for ambiguity manifests itself in a person's ability to operate effectively in an uncertain environment. A good amount of ambiguity tolerance in general can not only help to take chances and make connections, but also helps to navigate an increasingly complex and dynamic work environment (103).

    o **Listening actively and asking open questions** to start dialogue and continue conversations. Such skills also make others feel valued and more willing to open up and share experiences.

- o **Thinking in synergies** enables sharing, learning and focuses the mind on collaboration, rather than competition. Every time ideas are shared with others and discussions arise, be they face to face or digitally, ideas are improved on, accelerated, new solutions considered, and innovations created.
- For leveraging contacts and working in groups either face-to-face or virtually, great communication skills, teamwork and a digital mindset are essential, as already covered.
- For contributing quality content, especially to online communities for extended reach, media competencies also require fine tuning.

> *The nature of humans is that they need to build alliances.*
>
>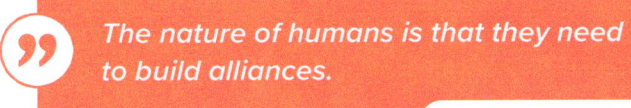

POSITIVE ONLINE PRESENCE THROUGH ONLINE ETIQUETTE

Good online presence is all about the mix of digital and media skills to create, publish and share information with a much wider internal or external audience. What is also important to understand is appropriate online behaviour is essential (104). How you behave in the online, and offline, world relates to attitude, a key success factor in business, yet one that cannot be easily changed. What can be developed is **appropriateness**. You can work to improve your personal brand or digital image. For example, the quality of posted material reflects your focus, ambition and professionalism. If you venture into the live online world of video or webinars, a webcam background is now part of a new digital image. For any home working, if you want to seem in control, don't be seen to take calls in the kitchen!

You can also choose to keep learning. Before remote or digital working, it mattered a lot if you were nice, effective and pleasant to work with. But if you're digitally illiterate, nice is not enough anymore – it's about taking technology seriously and learning how to use it.

Lastly, consider how you treat others. Nobody tries to be a moron when it comes to technology. We all do our best - even the person who has a feedback loop echo on the video call every day. Be kind online and in virtual meetings. Risk areas to be aware of include what you write, how you participate in online platforms, how you include others in online discussions and how you behave in live online sessions. Establish rules, keep structure and agendas, use technology well, contribute actively, be relevant and timely, be inclusive and be generous.

The **mind set for digital communication and virtual collaboration** includes the willingness to integrate everyone and actively include and integrate all participants to build real trust. This is true not only for meetings to inform but also engaging in discussions, taking time to ask others for input and empowering them get involved and take initiative. It can show that the group really is in this together. Secondly, always avoid limiting thinking and negatives of distance, such as isolation, taking time for people is vital. ... it is so easy to forget what's going on when you are miles apart. More effort is required to overcome assumptions, embrace diversity or different cultures, and take time for effective group work. Thirdly, it is the technology itself that makes digital communication, virtual collaboration and extended reach possible! And as Matt Mullenweg, Social Media Entrepreneur said, "technology is best when it brings people together" (105).

Summary of Connecting and Influencing Across the Organization and Beyond

Concept Level	Audience scenario	Goal	Communication Characteristics			Models	Additional virtual considerations
			Skills	Mindset	Presence		
Reach	Wider organization & external reach	Access for others and personal visibility & credibility	- Sharing ideas & information - Mixing the synchronous and asynchronous - Planning content & media / tool use - Emotional intelligence	- Mass sharing - Relationships & identity - Collaboration not competition - Digital use	- Investing time - Online & social media - Networking - Personal brand	- BRIEF - AIDA - 2-way tools - Depth versus range - Network dimensions	- Timeliness - Two-way response elements - Safe forum participation

PART 2

The Overarching Principle of Communication (The Deep Dive)

Welcome to part two of this compendium for genuine communication. Here we will take a deep dive into the principle of communication by reviewing what you must know and what you need to work on for great communication. We will also provide an overview of key tools and reflection exercises for transferring learnings to daily work. There are also some self-check examples that colleagues have shared with us from their personal learning journeys. The point is, communication can be learnt, and we will start there.

Chapter 6:

WHAT YOU NEED TO KNOW

Key knowledge

- Great communication can be learnt
- Key to adult learning is self-reflection, real-life experiences and having self-check mechanisms to avoid derailing behaviours
- Great communication is essential to foster trust and build relationships

Key models

- Adult learning process is iterative
- 70/20/10 learning concept emphasises the mix of learning opportunities
- Trust model describes how to achieve employee engagement and commitment through great communication, positive influence and creating a safe working environment
- Characteristics of great communicators include skills, mindset and presence
- Emotional intelligence is at the heart of being able to connect with others

Impact

- An organization born of trust is one where all feel positive, connected and appreciated and all employees contribute to business results

Knowledge is the awareness or understanding of a subject or topic, yet in general, our awareness or understanding of communication is limited. It is not always based on facts, nor is it planned as a process and it often lacks context. So, despite the truth that communication is as natural as breathing, like breathing it becomes subconscious or habitual and can often go wrong when we simply react or make quick, unthought through responses. We also underestimate the impact our communication has on other people. Only when we meet challenges and conflicts do we stop and think about new ways of behaving or consider how to communicate better. As leadership really is communication, to be a great leader, you must be a great communicator. Key is iterative learning, a focus on trust and choosing to care about being a great communicator.

THE GOOD NEWS IS COMMUNICATION SKILLS CAN BE LEARNT

Continuous learning is itself a competency, a transferable ability associated with higher potential for success in unknown situations, new roles and as a leader (42). In terms of adult learning, the most significant element is you! The responsibility for learning is yours.

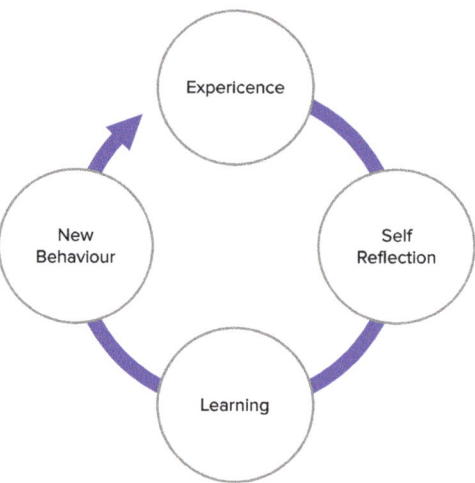

Figure 22: The adult learning process

Learning is a process, but one completely reliant on the learner for success.

Step one – an experience, such as an event at work, reading a paper or attending a training. These may provide new ideas, inputs, knowledge. They do not mean anything new happens though.

Step two is self-reflection – this means actively taking time to consider what the skill or knowledge gap was, what went well or could have been better. Reflection can be aided by feedback, however in general it is only an individual who can choose to invest energy here.

Step three is the eureka moment, the actual learning – determining what needs to be done differently, what to change or how to do something better.

Step four is also active – to apply the learning, try out a new skill or a new behaviour, have the courage to change.

When it comes to learning how to communicate better, it is essential to invest time and energy in reflection. Self-awareness is a key starting point for having a conscious knowledge of ourselves, including the ability to form an accurate self-concept and understand the impact we have on others. Self-reflection is fundamental in considering your own role in situations and showing willingness to seek feedback. Self-reflection makes self-responsibility possible. By analyzing your reactions to certain trigger, you can start to self-check and avoid old habits. Only when you take responsibility for personal actions can you truly develop appropriateness towards others and continue to learn and grow. It also requires admission of mistakes and clearing up miscommunications when necessary.

Reflection Task	Personal notes
How would you rate your current communication ability?	
What are you best at as a communicator?	
What positive feedback have you received about your communication?	
What negative feedback have you received?	
Are you aware how your emotions influence your behaviour?	
Can you identify how negative or hurtful behaviour triggers your emotions?	
Are you aware of the impact you have on others when you communicate?	
Are you able to influence others positively and build rapport?	
Do you take time to plan your communications?	
Do you reflect upon your role when communication goes wrong?	
Do you have goals for your personal development?	
What do you need to work on to be a better communicator?	
How can you practice being a better communicator?	

LEARNING COMES FROM REAL-LIFE EXPERIENCES

The second bit of good news for learning how to be a better communicator is that every event, good or bad, can help you, so long as you are willing to reflect, figure out what to change and then try it out. Learning is iterative and learning is lifelong.

The 70/20/10 learning concept model highlights that learning is not about training! 70% of what we learn happens "on the job" and 20% we pick up from observing others or working with great role models. With this knowledge, every day is an opportunity to grow and be an even better communicator. Look for trends in your behaviour and responses, make notes when things go well or not, set goals, plan more, apply models and continue to reflect.

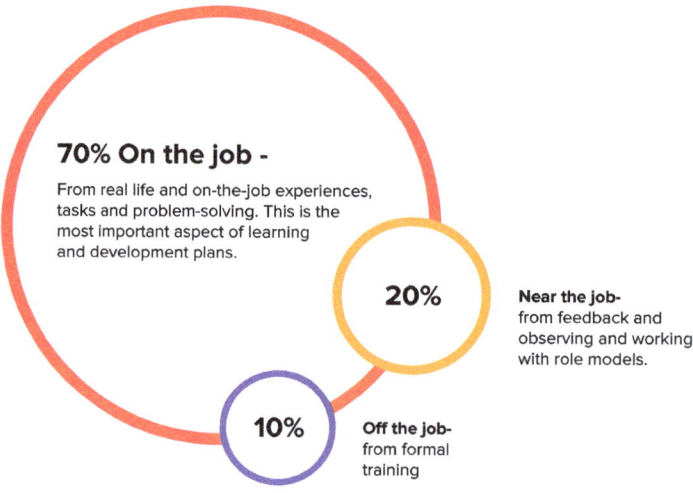

Figure 23: The 70/20/10 learning concept (106)

UNDERSTANDING THE SECRET OF TRUST

The key goals of communication are to build relationships and connect with others. This therefore puts trust at the centre of communication. Trust is also the precursor to positive engagement and organizational commitment (6, 107, 108, 109). Trust is fostered through great communication, positive influence and creating a safe environment in which others can thrive. When you get this right in the workplace, what you achieve are relationships that are resilient to crisis, the power to shift behaviours, beliefs or opinions, and dedication from employees. Not only is trust the key, trust is also a duty (32). From trust, engagement, active participation in work tasks is built. From here, commitment is possible, meaning employee dedication to tasks, projects and the organization.

> *Organizations are no longer built on force but on trust. The existence of trust between people does not necessarily mean that they like each other. It means they understand one another. Taking responsibility for relationships is therefore an absolute necessity. It is a duty.*
>
> Peter Drucker (32)

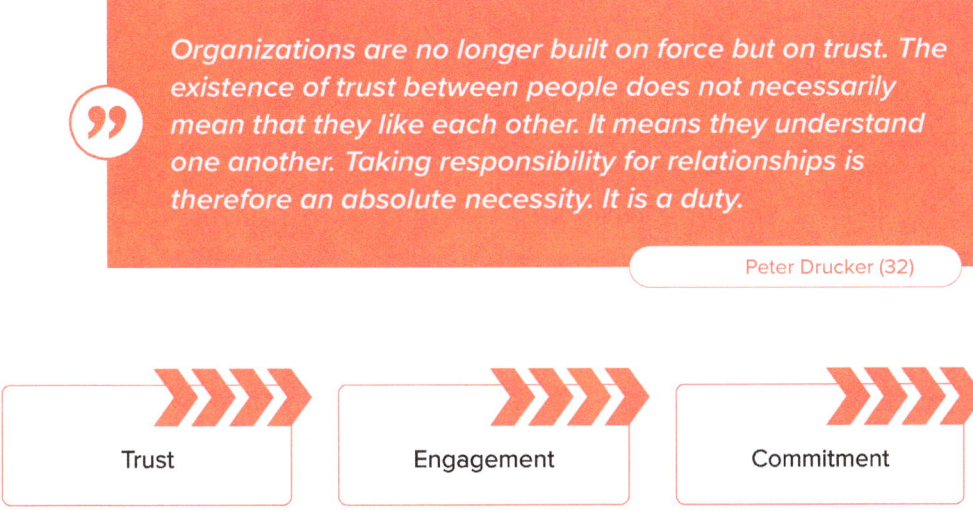

Fostered through:
Great Communication - Positive Influence - Safe Environment

Figure 24: Trust as the precursor to engagement and organizational commitment

What exactly is trust? Trust is defined as "a state comprising the intention to accept vulnerability based upon positive expectations of the intentions or behaviour of another" (110). In other words, **allowing vulnerability**, to speak openly about a mistake for example, because the expectation is that the other person will react in a positive way. The goal of trust is therefore to create an environment of openness and honesty, allowing people to show their weaknesses as well as strengths, without fear of recrimination or abuse.

Trust is also a principle of effective management (35). Management is a process to produce order and consistency by being highly task oriented and focused on goal setting and control. Effective management plays a very important role in business success and one principle is trust. Especially in the virtual world where managers cannot see their employees, increasing levels of trust are required, not increasing levels of control! Trust is the reason why managers can be successful even when they make mistakes and conflicts or difficulties can be solved, based on existing trustful relationships.

When we trust someone, we have **confidence in them** and in their honesty and integrity. We believe that they will do the things they say they will. We recognize their abilities and strengths, and we place our faith in them. Building up mutual trust in a team comes from how leaders treat individuals and how mistakes are used as learning experiences, not for punishment. To generate trust, you need to listen empathetically, be authentic and act according to what you say. Shared values, manners and respect for all are fundamental. In general, trust is what individuals reflect back. Hence it starts by being open and transparent; being dependable, consistent, and reliable; and taking responsibility when things don't work out quite as planned. As Simon Sinek simply put it, "to build trust, tell the truth" (16).

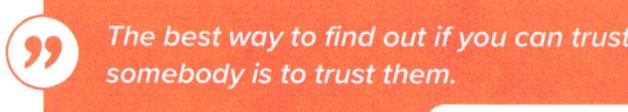

The best way to find out if you can trust somebody is to trust them.

Ernest Hemingway (111)

HOW TO BUILD TRUST THROUGH GREAT COMMUNICATION

From the five reasons communication goes wrong, the 5 axioms (see chapter 1), we know that every communication has a content and relationship aspect (14) and trust works on this relationship aspect as it has an impact on how we perceive the other person. Trust and commitment do not just happen; they are forged and maintained through communication by leaders (6) and research shows:

- Leader's ability to listen and communicate clearly has the strongest effect on employees' organizational commitment
- The perception of effective communication affects a company's trust climate
- When communication deteriorates or fails, misunderstandings and misrepresentations abound, and mistrust sets in
- To build trust, communication must be honest and direct, particularly during uncertain times

If trust is an intention to demonstrate openness to others, enabling **engagement** in activities and **commitment** from employees, how can communication be used to achieve such mighty heights? It comes down to the quality of the communication people receive from the organization as a whole, and more importantly, individual leaders and managers. To build trust, employees seek timely, accurate and useful information (7). With this in mind, there are five main aspects to include when planning great communication, with the goal of inspiring, connecting and building relationships.

The 5 key aspects in creating great communication strategies:
1. Imparting an inspiring shared vision with others so they understand why they are there, why they should listen or what's in it for them (why)
2. Creating audience-centric content / messages, using language all understand (relevant)
3. Combining different methods and tools for delivery such as mixing presentations, white board use, documents, digital tools, data, graphs, images (memorable)
4. Allowing for multi-directional, formal and informal settings to create dialogue (interactive)
5. Including positive and negative information, especially when communicating complex topics or change (believable)

Even as an individual team leader or project manager, you can create a **vision for others** relating to activity focus or project outcomes, because a vision describes, in writing, long term aims and direction. A good vision however creates a mental picture so also has access to unconscious needs and motivators (112), therefore has the power to inspire and direct actions. So not only should a team or project vision be a positive, emotionally charged image of a desirable future, it should be an achievable future for the audience. As a vision can be considered a compass, setting future direction, aligning efforts and focusing on significant goals, it answers big questions on why we care or bother, in other words, engaging people what they do and why they do it. At best, an inspiring image wins hearts and minds. It also supports the communication necessary to transition from trust to positive engagement to organizational commitment.

> *Efforts and courage are not enough without purpose and direction.*
>
> John F Kennedy (113)

HOW TRUST LEADS TO INFLUENCE

From an internal communication perspective, well developed and effective communication requires the use of different skills and tools to deliver consistent, impactful and inspiring messages in different scenarios. For example, as a manager, in one-to-one situations genuine focus is placed to engage the other party. In group meetings, it's about actively leading discussions and facilitating outcomes to integrate all members to meet shared goals. Finally, to reach a wider organizational setting, written formats become paramount to inform or influence more broadly. Why must you be aware of these differences? It is because you need to be clear on what you are trying to achieve. Communication informs, builds trust and relationships and it is also the cornerstone of how we influence others!

Impact is to have a marked effect on someone or something, yet **influence** is the power to cause someone to change a behaviour, belief, or opinion, based on motivation and common vision (18). Influence is also different from persuasion (19). Persuasion, like coercion, is all about creating a desire in others to follow or say yes, a spur to action, however it includes obligations to give back. Influence on the other hand seeks long term and genuine buy-in to a vision or aligned goals to affect a change, it includes earning **sincere buy-in**.

We all have the ability to influence others. Whether it's in the workplace or at home, our actions influence other people's perception, feelings and thoughts. Because of this, you need to be careful in what you say and do. Managers especially need to be more mindful and pay attention to themselves as they can make other people be feel better or worse.

> *Nothing is as fast as the speed of trust. Nothing is as fulfilling as a relationship of trust. Nothing is as inspiring as an offering of trust. Nothing is as profitable as the economics of trust. Nothing has more influence than a reputation of trust.*
>
> Stephen Covey (46)

So, **influence is the power to have an effect on people**, or to cause something to be changed. It starts from having a vision of the optimum outcome for a situation or organization and then, without using force or coercion, motivating people to work together toward making the vision a reality. Behaviours that are impacted by positive influence include decision making and problem-solving, enabling more collaborative and creative approaches. This is critical for more flexible project work for instance, due to more reliance on informal leadership approaches, because influence is not linked to hierarchy.

There are many elements that affect an individual's ability to influence in the workplace. These can include:

- Communication, as well as how individuals come across, their presence or business persona
- Whether they are credible, based on skills, knowledge and expertise
- If they are known for having a proven track record for performance and delivery
- Who they know, who they are networked with and how they form coalitions
- If they are seen to respect and value differences, and actively consider the interests of others
- Their awareness for and respect for power structures

There may be others, dependent on the situation and individuals involved. However, the core elements of influence can be narrowed to power, trust and understanding (114), as these frame relationships. In time-sensitive circumstances, persuasion may be useful for expediting results, however, in most situations, influence is the preferred means to a productive end. This is because influence is based on trustful relationships that have been solidified over time. It is all connected.

As said, trust is the basis and prerequisite for engagement, commitment, as well as influence. **Power** cannot be ignored as it is part of all communication and relationships (14) and is the ability to create behaviours in others which they would not have shown by themselves. Power facilitates decision making and those deciding set future direction. It is also associated with responsibility, yet it does create boundaries. Linked to the axioms of communication, asymmetric power can be a reason why communication goes wrong and more often than not, communication between equals works better (14). As a manager, formal hierarchic power is given, however should not be used to coerce. Instead managers and leaders need to be cognitive of building influence via personal types of power (115). Referent power for example, comes from being trusted and respected for what we do and how we handle situations.

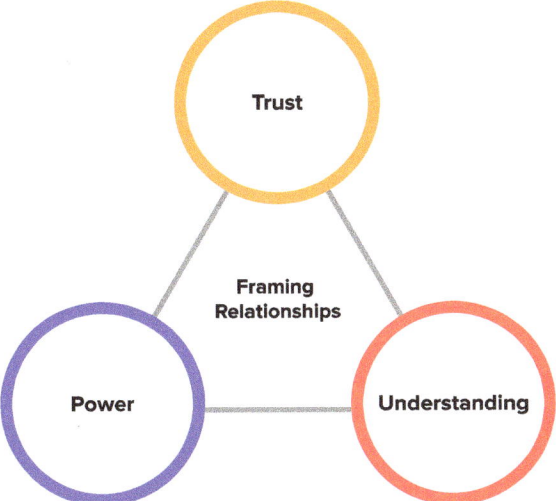

Figure 25: The 3 core elements of influence (114)

Expert power comes from our experience, skills or knowledge and how that is also utilized by others. Lastly, understanding others to create common ground and acceptance is key to having a vision of an optimum outcome for all, and moving towards that shared vision, even when starting goals may be different. Seeking to understand others is a cornerstone of great communication, begun by asking questions, listening and entering genuine dialogue.

Taking these 3 elements into account, **influence really does come down to communication** - it is communicating in a way that shows respect for all people, shows understanding of the interests of others, seeks to integrate and incorporate their needs and therefore inspires others to act. What becomes important is understanding who you wish to influence and then how best to do it for them.

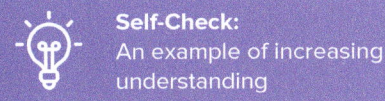

Self-Check:
An example of increasing understanding

"It's when I am quiet and just listen..."

TRUST AND SAFETY

Influencing others and getting the best out of others can also be considered part of making employees feel positive, connected and appreciated. When understanding how to do this better, demonstrating appreciation of others maintains motivation and commitment. It has been shown that people need encouragement to function at their best and to keep going over long periods when the hours are long, the work is hard, and the task is challenging (27). Leaders who remember to say "thank you" to people who work for them find that those employees feel motivated to work harder (48). To achieve such results, it has also been shown that **psychological safety** is a critical success factor. This topic is highly relevant for leaders to ensure they understand each person in a team and can enable each member to be in the best frame of mind for performance. Specifically, on the communication theme, once a team feels secure, they are more willing to speak up, contribute and gains sense of belonging, even if they are miles apart and working remotely. One element of such safety is also trust.

Before looking more into psychological safety, let's consider psychological threat. Have you ever felt overcome with emotions or thoughts that made you feel marginalized, rejected, alienated or hopeless? Or experienced physical sensations such as elevated pulse and churning in your stomach? Such an event can be brought on to varying degrees by perceived attacks on self-esteem, belonging, freedom, or sense of fairness for example. When you experience this, it is an attack to your psychological safety and your brain triggers a stress response that derails thinking and impacts productivity in the workplace. Neuroscience research (117) has shown that psychological pain, such as social rejection, can have a deeper and longer-lasting impact than physical pain.

On the flip side, **psychological safety in the workplace** means being able to show one's self without fear of negative consequences of self-image, status or career (118). It is related to belief that you will not be punished or humiliated for speaking up with ideas, questions, concerns, or mistakes (119). Research into teams at Google (120) has highlighted that such a safe climate means team members are not afraid to express themselves, feel accepted and respected. An environment for thinking, creativity, innovation and growth exists. Collaborative relationships are formed and overall results in enhanced productivity.

To consider how a leader can leverage knowledge in this relatively new field, and create safe and productive environments in which all can thrive (121), we will look at 3 parts:
- Understanding the neuroscience to reinforce why this topic is so important
- Reviewing common factors that threaten many people and cause them to feel unsafe
- Looking at how to create team safety

The Science - The brain is designed for safety and establishes patterns of reactions to keep us safe. The amygdala, the oldest part of the human brain, controls this drive for safety. When stimulated by physical threat the fight, flight, freeze survival instinct takes over to protect us. It is a very fast, emotional and subconscious reaction. However, the brain also perceives and responds to psychological threat in the same way and this can include relatively harmless situations like pressure from too many emails or looming deadlines. What we experience is stress. Stress is a normal short-term reaction to a threat or situation to enhance alertness, focus and performance, however if prolonged, can led to feeling overwhelmed and reducing performance.

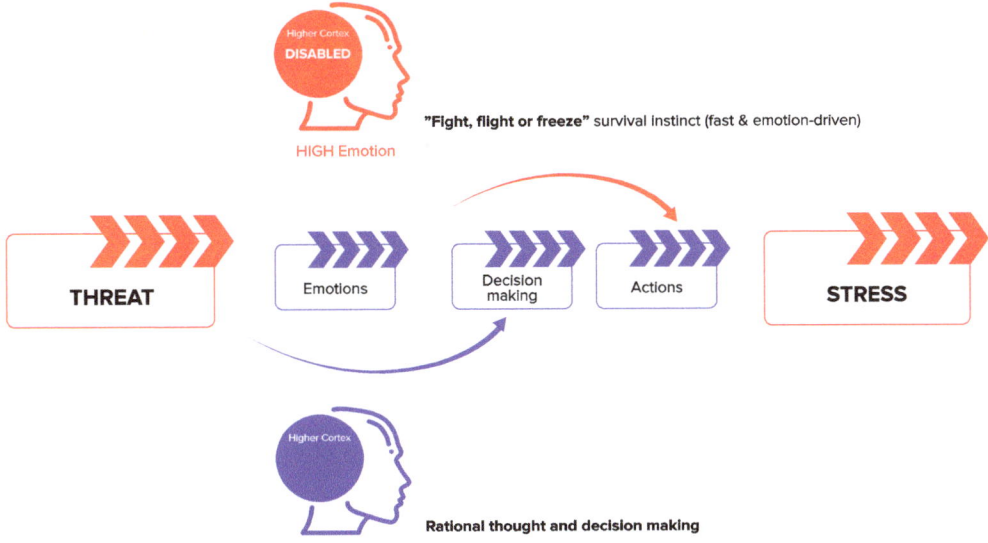

Figure 26: The science of psychological safety (121, 18)

Overcoming this natural negative bias towards threats requires us to override the fast-instinctive response and use our higher brain functions for conscious and logical thinking and decision making. In other words, we need to be aware of what **triggers** our sense of threat, be aware of being agitated by small annoyances, because if we don't, we do not feel safe and are less productive. When we engage our thinking brain, we can be analytical, creative, self-regulated, understand perspective and remain in the driving seat of our own reactions for better actions and performance. This is where we need to be as a leader and where leaders need their employees to be.

The Factors - To be in a climate of psychological safety it is important to know what threats can trigger the negative responses just described, to reduce or manage their impacts. Six important social factors have been defined that can trigger the threat response, hijack the brain and cause people to feel unsafe (121).

- Security is the need for predictability, consistency, commitment and certainty.
- Autonomy is the need to feel we have control over our environment and have choices.
- Fairness considers our need to engage in and experience fair exchanges for ourselves and others.
- Esteem considers our need to be regarded highly.
- Trust in team looks at the social need to belong to and protect our group.
- Personal Factors, unique for each individual also play a part and can be related to personality, personal biases and personal influences.

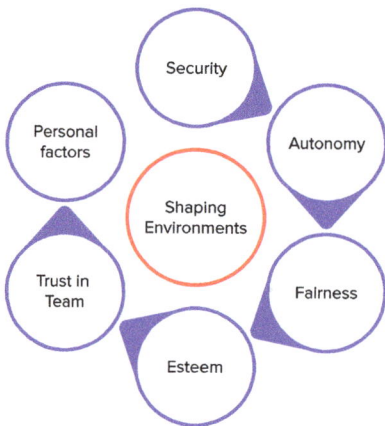

Figure 27: The 6 social factors of psychological safety (121)

Team Safety - Finally, let's look at how to create team safety to achieve a team that is open, not afraid to admit mistakes and willing to speak up or take risks. As a leader, it may be difficult to uncover the motives of each individual in the team, however understanding situations that may trigger safety concerns and common trigger issues, can help alleviate frictions, conflicts and genuine fears. For example, large organizational changes and uncertainty will threaten many with high security needs. Those who value autonomy will underperform when subjected to micromanagement and over control. Scapegoating would anger many in teams who are driven by fairness and exclusion from the inner circle would threaten many who need the sense of belonging. Recognition is a simple way you can make workers feel valued and regarded, but imagine a remote worker missing such recognition simply because they are far way. Individual factors may be harder to consider, yet time spent getting to know employees will help build a better understanding of individuals, as well as establish the relationship for trust, influence and psychological safety.

Tips for creating a safe environment for those with high or lower needs in each area:	
Security: **High need:** Provide details; over-communicate about expectations and potential risks; allow space for lots of questions; minimise changes/ambiguity **Low need:** Give new / risky assignments; limit rules; give freedom to explore opportunities	**Autonomy:** **High need:** Give freedom to operate independently; avoid advising unless asked; offer choice, never ultimatums; give responsibility **Low need:** Give clear direction and feedback; don't push for opinions or decision making
Fairness: **High need:** Transparent policies for all; fulfil expectations; avoid favouritism; allow all to contribute; avoid unearned rewards; respect relationships **Low need:** Focus on outcomes not political correctness, process or methods	**Esteem:** **High need:** Praise and recognise in public; deliver criticism carefully; motivate with status gains; avoid one-upmanship / competition **Low need:** Praise and recognise in private; avoid comparing to others or peer pressure
Trust in team: **High need:** Use "we" language; connect personally; show loyalty and empathy; engage people collaboratively **Low need:** Don't force group work, allow solo projects; respect non-compliance to rituals/norms	**Personal factors:** Take time to connect with people. Treat people as individuals. Leverage and develop strengths. Value differences. Actively include all.

TRUST IS ESSENTIAL IN VIRTUAL SCENARIOS

For any job, you need skills and competencies and in virtual environments, even more skills are required to connect with people not physically present. For effective communication more focus is placed on skills for expressing ideas, facts, information more consistently and in formats appropriate for remote workers, combining calls, online meetings, email, chat etc. Choosing appropriate language and emotional connections to engage others, to motivate and inspire also requires added effort by leaders.

The mindset for virtual communication and collaboration also requires more willingness to integrate and actively include all team members. Firstly, this requires digging even deeper to build real **trust** by getting to know individuals and avoiding asymmetric power. Secondly, to reduce the effects of distance, separation and isolation, taking extra **time** with people is vital, so more time needed for discussion, uncovering hidden reactions and overcoming missing non-verbal clues. It is so easy to forget what's going on when you are miles apart, hence repetition is required. Thirdly, it is the **technology** itself that makes virtual communication possible. So, in the virtual world, trust, time and technology are the secrets of connectedness!

Key Learning Points on Trust

- Two-way trust is required in any organization as the precursor to employee engagement and commitment. It is fostered by leaders through great communication, positive influence and creating a safety environment
- For communication to build trust it must impart an inspiring vision for future direction, be audience-centric, mix delivery methods and tools, include interactive and informal parts (not just one-directional) and be honest / believable (include negative truths)
- Trust is a core element of influence
- Influence is having a positive effect on someone else such that they willingly buy-in to a concept, goal or vision.
- For communication to build influence it must show respect for people, show understanding of others' interests and integrate others' perspectives. This only happens when a strong relationship exists and formal, directive power is not used
- Willingness to work hard requires employees to feel appreciated and psychologically safe. Leaders can create a sense of team safety to enhance relationships and collaborations
- Trust is a factor in psychological safety
- For communication to build sense of safety it must balance individuals' needs for trust, security, autonomy, fairness and esteem
- Trust, not control, is more important in virtual scenarios where distance may limit relationships and cause feelings of isolation

Reflection Task	Personal notes
Is your approach to work, life and people based on trust or control?	
Would others describe you as trustworthy?	
How do you set about to create trust at work?	
Is power, status and winning your primary driver?	
Do you take time to really understand other people?	
Can you balance risk and ambiguity, so others feel safe?	
Are you careful to respect and build esteem in others?	
Do you react strongly when you believe others are being treated unfairly?	
Are you aware of your biases and own assumptions?	
When do you judge others more negatively than you should?	
What situations make you feel uncomfortable?	
Do you take responsibility for the impact you have on others?	
How can you demonstrate more trust and create a safe environment in which others can thrive?	

UNDERSTANDING THE CHARACTERISTICS OF GREAT COMMUNICATORS

Great communicators are first and foremost, individuals who to choose to care about how they communicate, not how important they appear, but how they positively influence others and make others feel. The characteristics of such people include a combination of skills, mindset and presence and their intention is to connect with and engage someone else, not make their point or simply try to win. They demonstrate curiosity to increase understanding of themselves and others, courage to keep going when things are tough, and show kindness to others at all times.

Key elements of the skills, mindset and presence are covered in detail in subsequent chapters. Here we will dive deeper into the central element, emotional intelligence, and the link between personal values, emotions, thoughts and actions, including how we choose to communicate.

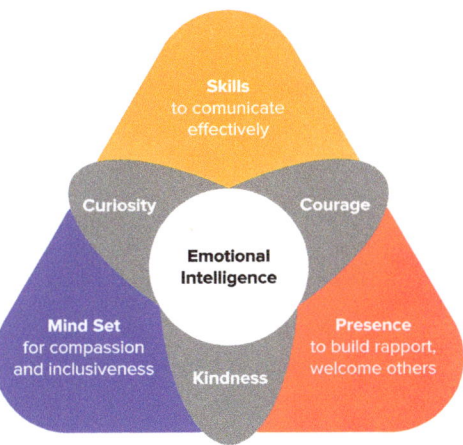

Figure 28: Characteristics of great communicators

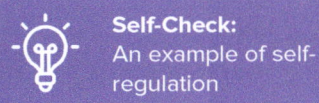

Self-Check:
An example of self-regulation

"It's when I pause and pay attention..."

EMOTIONAL INTELLIGENCE FOR GREATER CONNECTEDNESS

As we touched on in chapter 2, emotional intelligence is the understanding of and managing your own emotions and those of the people around you for greater connectedness. It impacts your ability to project an authentic, professional yet caring manner, portraying a style of communication most effective in any given situation, building rapport and building relationships. In the workplace, if you wish to be a great communicator and desire influence, you must know yourself, how you come across and how you interact with others.

Just as ripples spread out when a single pebble is dropped into water, the actions of individuals can have far-reaching effects

Dalai Lama (122)

Looking at yourself starts with understanding personal drivers to see how what you express to others is driven by our own values and motives, and how you feel and think. **Values** are your principles of behaviour or judgement of what is important in life, and **motives** are what make you tick. For example, intrinsic motivations guide your career choices and define the activities you like to do (123). How you like to do things is the translation of your values, feelings and thinking, through to your behaviours. Specifically, in the business context, feelings can be regarded by assessing emotional intelligence or emotional competencies. Visible behaviours, such as what you say or do, can be seen as your communication style.

The link between how you feel, what you think and how you act is extremely powerful and important as your actions impacts others. The biggest challenge is the power of unchecked emotions, especially under stress. The moment you lose emotional control, you lose the ability for good decision making, effective communication and therefore positive influence. Emotional competencies are proven to be crucial for effective communication as they predict how you deal with your own and other's feelings, anticipate reactions and understand how to be effective in social, stressful or emotional situations. Strong emotional intelligence and balanced emotional competencies are essential for leaders.

The Science – Similar to understanding psychological threats, emotions can also have a physiological effect before you understand what you feel and can therefore hijack rational thinking and result in poor actions (11). The amygdala and prefrontal cortex of the brain both support processes that are important for the expression and regulation of the emotional response to stress (124). Though there is individual variability in stress responses, for many, in high emotional states the complex prefrontal cortex shuts down and the amygdala takes over for rapid reactions. This fight, flight or freeze survival instinct is still very powerful and if left unchecked can lead to poor reactions. On the other hand, those with high emotional intelligence are able to overcome this quick impulsive response and employ rational thought, such as in low emotional states, when the prefrontal cortex can perceive, control and evaluate emotions and to use this information to guide thinking and actions. This is known as emotional separation, enabling inner calm in difficult circumstances and retention of the ability to think rationally and use relevant competencies in order to take high quality decisions and then act or communicate in the best way.

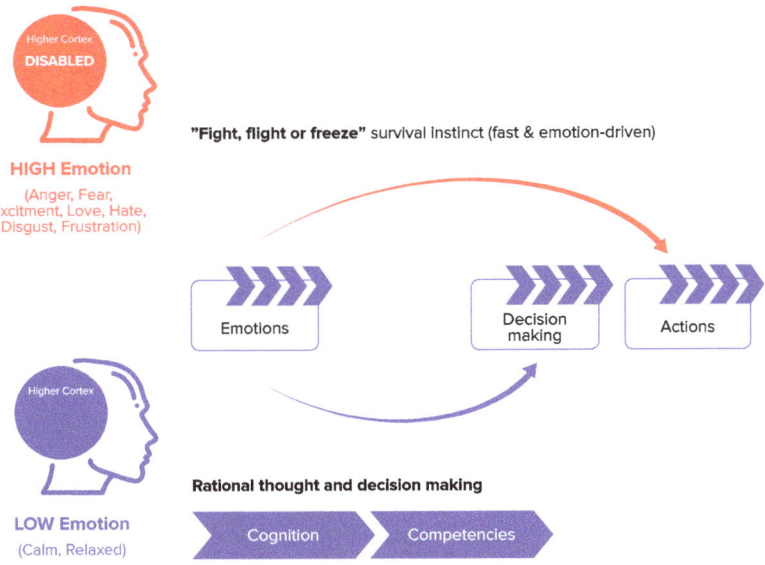

Figure 29: The science of emotional intelligence

In summary, emotional intelligence refers to the ability to perceive, control and evaluate emotions and Goleman, the "father" of emotional intelligence, defined 5 elements to frame this ability towards self and other people (11).

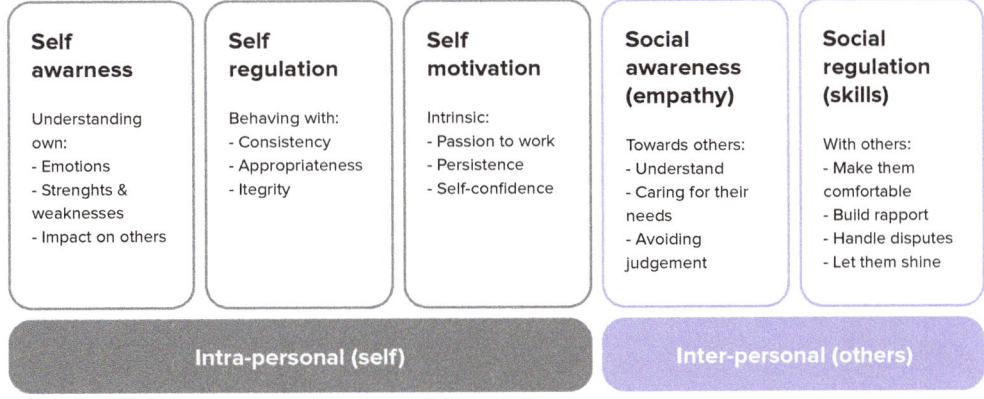

Figure 30: The elements of emotional intelligence

What someone with high emotional intelligence can do is think before they act or speak. By doing so, they are preventing a quick, emotional response, evaluating a situation, and choosing a style of response and appropriate language for a better outcome. Critically, they are also able to behave and communicate well under **stress** or high-pressure work situations.

What can you learn? How can you improve your emotional intelligence for more successful interactions and collaborations, especially when under stress?

Tips for enhancing emotional intelligence elements for better communication with others:			
EQ Element	**Benefits**	**Dos**	**Don'ts**
Self-awareness	Realistic self-image	Admit weaknesses and mistakes. Act upon feedback.	Blame external factors for problems. Ignore how you affect other people.
Self-regulation	Able to manage stress, avoid outbursts	Pause, think & listen before acting. Consider alternative approaches. Know your mood shifters.	Make impulsive decisions or act when feeling mad, bad or sad. Take things personally.
Self-motivation	Confidence, intrinsically driven, not seeking approval or recognition from others	Find inner belief. Act with humility. Be open to changes and challenges, keep learning, set personal goals.	Demand recognition. Make winning everything. Get angry when you are not appreciated.
Social awareness (empathy)	Connecting with others, showing you care	Observe, listen & consider others. Treat all with respect. Be generous with time, feedback & info. Follow your intuition	Stereotype or judge others. Ignore other's input or concerns. Ignore other's feelings. Make assumptions.
Social regulation (social skills)	Connecting with others, building rapport and relationships	Be curious, excited, open & honest. Welcome people, address with names. Improve questioning & empathetic listening. Compromise, find solutions together. Positive body. language. Praise, let others shine.	Tell or insist on being right. Communicate only in "your way". Hide or ignore people or problems. Be distracted when talking to people. Hold grudges.

Key Learning Points on Great Communication Starts with You

- Great communication starts from choosing to care how you communicate and how you make others feel
- What you care about, how you feel, how you think and how you act are all connected
- Understanding how you and others feel is key to emotional intelligence
- High emotional intelligence predicts greater ability to build rapport and communicate well, even under stressful situations
- Emotional intelligence can be developed through the adult learning process

Reflection Task	Personal notes
What are your personal values and motives?	
How would you rate your emotional intelligence on each of the 5 elements? (could be better – good enough – excellent) • Self-awareness • Self-regulation • Self-motivation • Social-awareness (empathy) • Social-regulation (skills)	
What feedback have you had on your emotional intelligence?	
Do you take notice when emotions are taking over an interaction?	
How do you show a genuine curiosity for others' well-being?	
Do you allow others to take the lead role so you can learn from them?	
Do you seek learning from those above you or peers and other colleagues?	
Do you connect easily with people you just met, finding ways to build rapport?	
Do you seek quality, rather than quantity, in your social bonds?	
How do you converse with others on a deeper level at home?	
How do you converse with others on a deeper level at work?	
How can you develop your emotional intelligence to achieve greater social success?	

Chapter 7:

DEVELOPING YOUR SKILLS

Key knowledge

- Communication is a comprehensive competency, the most significant transferable ability enabling success in complex and unknown situations
- Highly developed skills allow communication to be inspiring, relevant, memorable, interactive and believable
- Communication is a process and all steps have risks and all steps can be improved

 Key models

- Planning: setting goals and following the process
- Content: language, tone and next steps
- Formats: mixed modalities of text, images, sound, interaction and body language
- Tools and channels: mixing synchronous and asynchronous tools specific for the audiences one-to-one, in groups or across the wider organization
- Adaptability: balancing own preferred style versus preferred style of someone else to communicate in a way that the other person is more receptive to

 Impact

- Communicating and behaving in a way that shows care for messages and care for the impact the messages have on others to ensure the best outcome in terms of understanding and action

Effective communication is also described as a meta-competency, an 'overarching' ability that is relevant to a wide range of work settings and which facilitates adaptation and flexibility especially in unknown or challenging situations. Communication is also a process with desired outcomes that easily go wrong without understanding, care or planning.

Here we will review what this all means and how best to plan appropriate content and format that audiences care about because their needs and perspectives are considered.

WHY IS COMMUNICATION SO CRITICAL AS A COMPETENCY?

For any job role, knowledge and qualifications are essential and developing new skills through training improves performance in a specific role. Competencies on the other hand are not role-specific but are transferable abilities which enable success in complex and unknown situations (125). As such they are better indicators of success and many organizations and employers seek to hire people who demonstrate certain competencies. Common core competencies many businesses desire include continuous learning, taking initiative, planning and problem solving, teamwork and accountability.

Effective communication transcends other competencies as it is critical for success with others. It is how you come across, your observable behaviour, and impacts employee engagement (42).

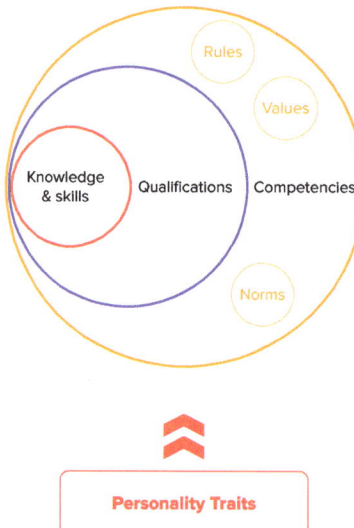

Knowledge & Qualifications:

- Focused on a specific skill/ expertise area

Competencies:

- Transferable abilities
- Enable success in complex, unknow situations

Figure 31: Understanding competencies (42)

Effective communication includes abilities to:

- Think with clarity
- Express ideas, facts and information consistently and inspirationally
- Choose appropriate language a multitude of differing audience types will best understand
- Handle the rapid flows of information within the organization, and among customers, partners, and other stakeholders and influencers
- Handle discrepancies and conflicts in a constructive manner
- Skills to support such outcomes include empathetic listening, engaging others in dialogue, asking questions, utilizing input/ideas from others, facilitating meetings, summarizing discussions, actively distributing clear information, presenting concepts and facts, and be inspiring emotionally
- In one-to-one settings behaviours include welcoming appropriately (handshake), creating a positive and respectful atmosphere, asking questions and listening, staying calm. It also includes showing empathy (empathetic dialogue), building rapport and conveying difficult messages with balance of positive and negative inputs so recipients are able to buy into the messages. Leading genuine conversations with open questions and appreciation and not back down when challenged is also required at times
- In group settings expected behaviour consists of willingness to speak up and influence the group, being able to get a message across, being accepted by the group and listened to. Can explain reasoning / thinking to get buy-in and checks others agree. Getting involved and actively contributing throughout the entire work process in groups is required and seeking to engage / include all, as well as other quieter team members by asking their opinion, asking specific questions, and following up is observed
- In formal presentations success comprises communicating ideas and opinions in a clear and comprehensible way, using good structure, key messages and a summary. Use of supportive body language, good voice modulation, ensures authentic and credible appearance. It is also expected to consider the audience (relevancy, appropriate level, language and detail) and demonstrate the ability to inspire, spread enthusiasm and create buy-in, for example by using stories, examples or images for impact. Overall, presentations have an agenda, follow a clear storyline and balance text versus graphical elements well.
- In written materials, expectations consist of succinct, structured, and appropriate mix of text, image, tables, graphs etc (modalities). Embracing digital literacy and use of effective technology for digital formats would be visible.

Communication is the one thing we all do day in and day out, yet often with little thought for the goal or the skills needed for effectiveness. Overall, the goal is to connect with and build relationships with individuals, teams and the wider organization. Communication is all about conveying meaning, about sharing information and affecting outcomes. How and what we communicate impacts our relationships, both personal and business, creates impressions, good or bad, and impacts our ability to positively influence others. Though we constantly communicate through our words, body language, written messages and images, effective communication is a learned skill that requires knowledge, application and continuous development.

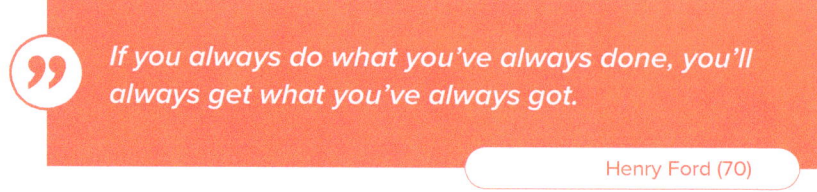

If you always do what you've always done, you'll always get what you've always got.

Henry Ford (70)

To begin to understand how to communicate well, it is important to understand the process of communication, with goals and outcomes, as well as the skills needed for proficiency.

UNDERSTANDING THE PROCESS OF COMMUNICATION

Communication is a process and should be understood as such, as processes, with steps in order to achieve a particular outcome, can go wrong. They can also be actively improved.

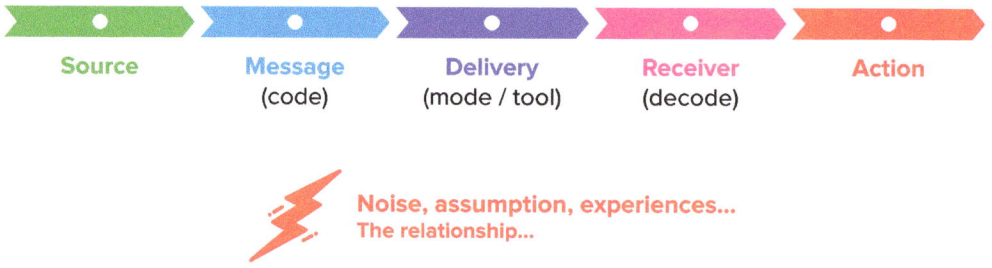

Figure 32: The communication process (127)

What this process view implies straight away is that sender and receiver need to use the same code or language to understand each other! When the receiver doesn't necessarily come to the same understanding as the sender, this leads to misunderstanding. This can happen due to message distortion from noise or incorrect assumptions, different experiences and even irritations in the relationship of sender and receiver. However, it is the responsibility of the sender to ensure the right message gets through – so it needs to be of interest, relevant and simple to understand and remember, possible to respond to, and believable.

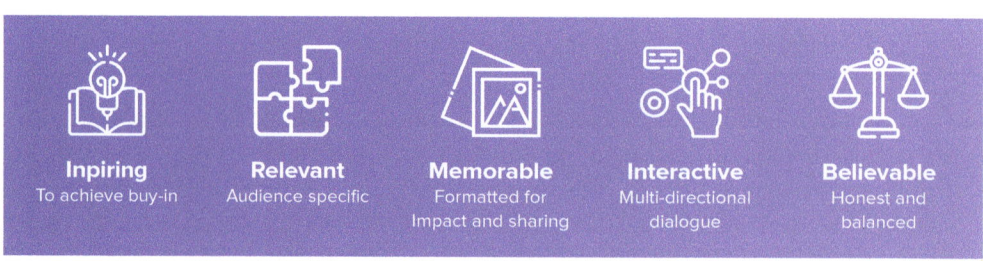

Figure 33: The 5 key aspects of great communication

To focus the sender on the real "message" that is to be gotten across, it helps to start with setting the communication goal or outcome desired. In the business world, managers are familiar with goal setting, the development of a plan designed to motivate and guide others towards a desired outcome. This structured cognitive approach can help shape the effectiveness of communication.

> **Key questions to always consider:**
> - What outcome do you want to achieve?
> - Have you provided all information the other person needs to make a decision for example?
> - Can you simplify or amend the communication to make it easier to understand and act upon?

PLANNING THE CONTENT FOR COMMUNICATION

Communication is so much more than facts, and messages must also go deeper than facts to be **inspiring** so people actual want to listen. As we looked at in chapter 4, inspiring communication is all about going beyond the everyday factual, detailed and operational work communication, to the part that links to emotions. To grab attention and engage others, is all about audience-relevant messages that are simple and short, and in the order people want to listen to, with the **"why" first**.

Taking communication to the emotional level also balances tone, imagery and next step elements. To create a sense of feeling, the **tone of a message** is important. For example, employees expect managers and leaders to convey optimism and confidence, share common purpose and express their personal commitment. Balanced facts give credibility to a message, making it more **believable**. An honest presentation of positive and negative information for example, upsides and downsides, as well as focus on future orientation or an external view such as the customer perspective also adds weight and believability. Emotional connections can also be strengthened through use of **images**, stories, metaphors, quotations or references. Finally, any communication message should also include a **what's next** – what you want people to do now....be specific on desired actions.

The words or text we choose are obviously a key aspect of great communication too – **language** counts. First and foremost, remember KISS – keep it short and simple! People only remember 25 - 50% of what they hear (69). Avoid jargon and acronyms as these can exclude rather than enable connecting to others. Also avoid "but". But is used to introduce a phrase contrasting with what has already been said and can end a statement or conversation on a very negative note. Especially when you are highlighting the positives, try to add, "... and it could be even better if......". Not only is it human to desire appreciation (47), focusing on peoples' strengths enables "optimal functioning, development and performance" (128).

In summary, is about creating audience-centric messages, in other words, **relevant** messages that focus on what matters to the "audience".

> **Audience-centric messages:**
> - Explaining the "why" first — specifically what it means to them.
> - Content mix of fact & emotion — can be through stories, images, examples or interactions.
> - Short & simple to avoid distraction or confusion — use familiar language, not jargon.
> - Clear next steps — so they understand the actions you want from them.

PLANNING THE DELIVERY FORMAT

Our messages are not only the words used, but are also coded in body language, written text and images. Remembering that our receptiveness (15) to others is only 7% from their words, and tone of voice is 38% and body language is 55%, senders need to ensure verbal and non-verbal signal alignment first. Body language counts! Secondly, mixed modalities or methods, also convey meaning in different ways and make messages more memorable.

Body language includes posture, gestures and eye contact. Simple positive signals include a real smile, good eye contact, leaning in towards someone, using reaffirming noises such as uh, ya..., and active participation in conversation. All shows warmth and genuine engagement. Negative or defensive signals can include broken eye contact, turning away at 45-90°, slouching, checking a watch or even sighing, arms crossed, leaning backwards and a blank face. Further disagreement signals include a set jaw, shaking head sideways and narrowed eyes. Remember **when the verbal / non-verbal don't match, this confuses people** and makes it difficult to understand the message and non-verbal communication is much stronger, more intuitive and more difficult to manipulate (14).

Body language is especially important in power and influence (129). Research shows that people posed in expansive postures feel more powerful, exhibit higher testosterone levels and have lower levels of the stress hormone cortisol — all characteristics of high-ranking social status (130). Making eye contact while talking, but feeling free to look away when others do, is called having a high "look-speak to look-listen ratio," which is also common for dominant members of groups. So, what we are talking about is presence as well as sending all the right signals.

With so much emphasis on body language what happens **when communication goes digital**? It is an obvious challenge and the answer is keeping the visual clues through video and using vocal clues as much as possible. Using **video** as much as possible keeps the eye contact, the facial expressions, gestures, posture and body orientation. When visible changes occur, something can be done. It's then about stopping, regrouping, asking what is not working, what is not understood. Without these signals, misunderstandings, frustrations and frictions can escalate.

Vocal clues can also give just as much meaning. When listening to understand, what people say and the language used, becomes more significant to sensing context or meaning. This includes clues on willingness to engage, openness to explain and sensitivity to consider the other person. For example, just making statements, talking in jargon or 3-letter acronyms does not suggest desire for dialogue. What they are not saying can also be inferred in other voice elements:

Tone – this suggests a person's mood and intention. Are they happy or sad?

Pitch – is speaking in a high, low or natural voice. Do they sound authentic or are they hiding something?

Pace – the speed at which someone speaks can alter during a conversation, such as the speed of response in an argument will go up.

Pause – a pause at a crucial moment could merit concern.

Volume – is important for audibility yet the effect of a loud, powerful voice or a quiet, nervous or sad voice may be more relevant.

Emphasis or stress on a particular word or phrase can change the meaning of a sentence as well as the feeling behind it.

Intonation – is the rise and fall of the voice. Generally, there is a clear movement up at the end of a sentence when we ask questions for example. Intonation also helps people say what they mean.

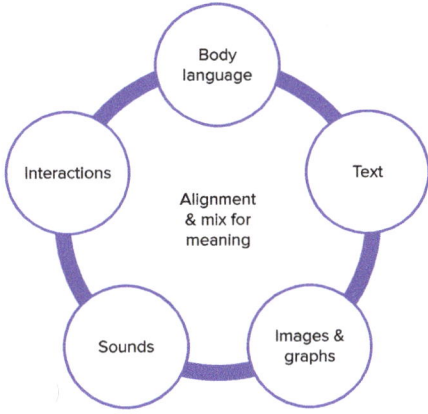

Figure 34: Mixed modalities or communication methods

Communication **modalities** are different ways, other than speech, that are used to convey meaning and stimulate all senses, so this can include body language, but also includes sign language, pictures, sound and writing. Cognitive psychologists have found that memory of a message is independent of the modality in which the information was delivered (18). Typically, memories are stored by meaning, not because information was seen, heard, or physically interacted with. However, when applied to learning, information or **content should be presented in its best modality**. For example, to appreciate the appearance of a pyramid, it would be much more effective to view a picture than to hear a verbal description. To truly appreciate a complex concept, a mix of modalities will be required to convey the full meaning, hence planning communication formats with text, images, sounds and interactive elements wherever possible. Choices can also be aligned with delivery tools for maximum effect. If images are required, a telephone call is not enough. Common **communication tools** in business still include mail, email, telephone, meetings and newer formats such as video conferencing and social media.

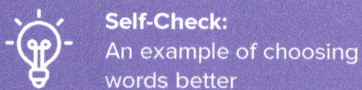

Self-Check:
An example of choosing words better

It's when I am more careful about the specificity of my language and what my words mean..."

PLANNING THE DELIVERY TOOLS OR CHANNELS

As we have mentioned in various chapters, the choice of tool(s) is very dependent upon the goal of the communication and in general, a mix of formats is best, allowing for consideration of modality, time span, depth of information, reach required and response elements.

Key is making communication **memorable** and useful, hence combining different methods and tools such as mixing presentations, white board use, documents, digital tools, data, graphs and images. In general, the more content-rich the communication, the more supporting documentation is also required.

Audience	Synchronous tools for exchange in real-time	Asynchronous tools with no immediate responses
One-to-one	Meeting, face-to-face or video Telephone calls	Chat tools Email & documents
Groups	Meeting, face-to-face or video Conference calls Events & workshops Webinars	Email & documents Information packages, brochures Project management systems Knowledge management systems
Wider organization or beyond	Company events Townhall meetings	Website Social media Online forum & networks

Figure 34: Mixed channels for information exchange

Making communication **interactive**, especially to build trust, is all about allowing multi-directional, formal and informal scenarios to create dialogue. Remember the key skill in dialogue is the ability to **ask questions and listening empathetically**. How to do this is covered in chapter 2.

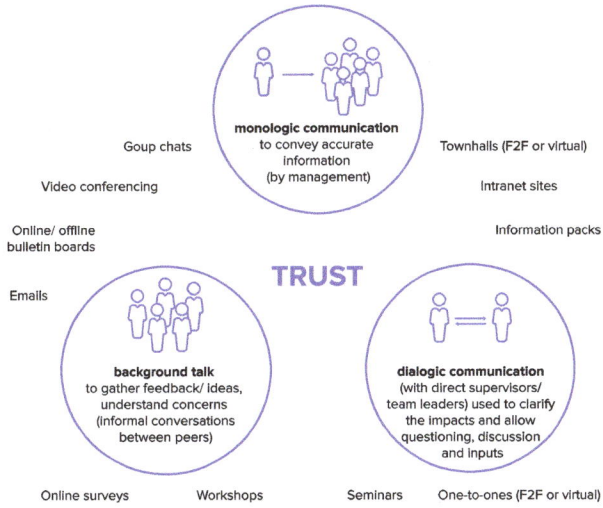

Figure 36: Mixed strategies for interactive reach

PLANNING FOR BROADER COMMUNICATION

When considering how to approach a more "mass" communication, a structured plan works best. Here are seven steps, to help create an effective media or communication concept that can be applied to reach wide audiences, either internal or external.

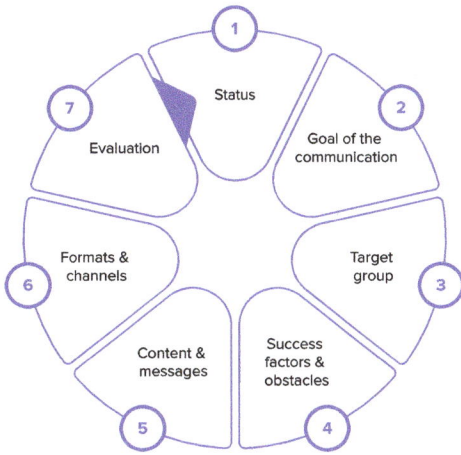

Figure 37: Seven steps for planning successful mass communication (131)

Step 1 - Consider the current situation. What is happening and what is already known.

Step 2 - What is the goal overall? Is it to share information, build relationships or establish identity?

Step 3 - Who are the target audiences? It is essential to understand that different groups of people need to be communicated with differently as their needs differ. If there are multiple groups to contact, otherwise known as stakeholders who have an interest in the topic, list them separately and review their needs separately. As an example, if you want to announce a new employee, stakeholders will include your team, key peer groups they will interact with, senior leaders, even customers if they will have interactions.

Step 4 - Consider what is vital to get right and what obstacles must be overcome. For example, if a common objection is already known, plan to address it head on.

Step 5 - From understanding all target groups (stakeholders), their needs and possible objections, define the content, wording, imagery etc for the communications. They will be different messages for different target groups. Keep it relevant to each of them.

Step 6 - How will the messages be delivered? What tools, channels or technologies will be employed to reach a broader network or achieve mass communication. This means defining the formats or channels such as online platforms, email, websites etc and the set plans in place to implement.

Step 7 - Lastly, how will the communication plan be evaluated? Were all target groups reached? Was the message understood? Were actions as desired? Were the goals met?

Following any such structure just means steps are not missed and the goals are more likely to be achieved.

OVERCOMING BARRIERS TO EFFECTIVE COMMUNICATION

Despite the vital need for highly effective communication in business, as well as our personal lives, skills and abilities in the area can still be a barrier, as can be too much or too little content or content not tailored for the receiver, messages full of jargon and inappropriate modalities (132). Individual senders also need to be willing to engage others in discourse to inform, appreciate, question, give and receive feedback and share visions, hopes and dreams. Limited ability or focus on only facts or communicating simply to inform, narrows the quality of dialogue and it all becomes one way, not two-way. Finally, lack of trust will always distort the message.

In **virtual environments**, the challenges and barriers to effective communication are even higher and require extra effort. It is easier when people are in the same room yet virtual communication and connecting to teams in our digital age is ever more paramount. In today's complex and global environment, leaders need to expand skills to communicate well. Leaders need to go beyond face-to-face leadership, into successful leadership of remote and virtual teams, including home workers. Leaders also need to go beyond their way of communicating and choose to care about who they are communicating with. One major aspect here is the willingness and ability to adapt.

WILLINGNESS TO ADAPT

Communication is not effective if people did not hear, understand or feel motivated to think differently and act differently as a result. Only when messages have an impact is there success. However, people listen from behind their own filters, perceptions or styles. This is why, to inspire and engage, communication needs to be about their concerns, their issues. This is what is meant by **audience-centric** communication, and recognizing that, when it comes to communication, it is all about the other person. A great communicator adapts their communication style depending on the audience and throughout a day, they may have to switch between styles to ensure the right message is received in the right way. It is not about being unauthentic, it is simply putting a message across in such a way that the receiver's needs or style is prioritized.

In chapter 3 we introduced the DISC methodology as a useful model for showing versatility or adaptability in communication styles (33). Here, we would like to encourage you to reflect upon and explore your own personal behavioural and communication style.

DISC considers two questions:

1. How do you make decisions? Using the vertical axis, please mark where you believe you lie. Are you more thinking and logical in your decision making, so nearer the top of the axis, or are you more feeling and emotional in your decision making, so nearer the bottom.
2. Where do you get energy? In other words, how do you refuel? Do you seek out the company of others and need people around you to re-energize, get excited by others? Extroverts, on the right of the horizontal axis need people around them to recharge. Introverts on the other hand prefer to refuel alone, to contemplate or recharge in more solitude and utilize more inner or self-energy. And yes, extroverts are more outgoing, more animated etc, whilst introverts can be quieter and more reflective. So, on the horizontal axis, please mark yourself.

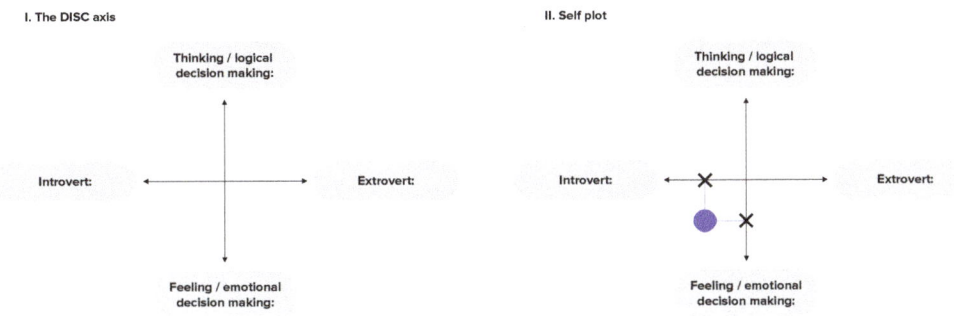

Figure 38: Finding where you lie on the DISC axis

From the reviews below, you can explore each profile to build of picture of the tendencies each has for communicating, as well as considering how this may appear to others, in other words the negative perceptions.

A Review of each DISC Profile:

A red or dominance profile

Describes someone fast, outgoing and task oriented who want results now. You appear proactive and decisive, you love challenges and new experiences and you tend to communicate in a very direct, but sometimes too telling manner.

Characteristics include:
- Taking initiative
- Independent
- Self-motivated
- Results focused

Limitations or negative perceptions from others:
- Lack tact, too blunt or dismissive of others' views
- Too demanding, even confrontational or aggressive
- Overly ambitious

A yellow or influence profile

Describes a lively person motivated by relationships, so you may be a strong networker, highly optimistic and futuristic. You love variety and discussing lots of ideas. Your style of communication is informal, wanting to connect to people before getting down to business. But be aware, because you like to discuss lots of ideas, you may appear unstructured to others.

Characteristics include:
- Self-confident
- Persuasive
- Popular & social
- Relationship oriented

Limitations or negative perceptions from others:
- Disorganized, poor finishers
- Too opinionated, even attention seeking
- Rebellious

A green or steadiness profile

Describes a quieter person yet a very strong team player who cares for others. You are dependable, supportive, loyal, systematic and a good listener, though not always willing to speak up in noisy environments and you need more reassurance in communications.

Characteristics include:
- Relaxed & patient
- Respectful
- Systematic
- Team oriented

Limitations or negative perceptions from others:
- Too modest, passive, even stubborn
- Slow decision makers,
- Overly cautious, resistant to change

A blue or compliance / conscientious profile

Describes a more serious person, motivated to act in environments of rules and procedures. As such you are detail oriented, analytical, accurate, and focused on quality. You want numbers, data and facts, are formal in communication yet need time to analyze to make rational choices. Be aware, for others, this can be perceived as slow and hindering quick actions.

Characteristics include:
- Contemplative
- Factual
- Precise
- Process oriented

Limitations or negative perceptions from others:
- Overly critical of self and others
- Restrained, hesitant, open to over-analyzing
- Evasive, withdrawn under pressure

From reflecting on the descriptions of each style, are you clear on your style? It is important you understand how you behave as this impacts the first impression you make and how others perceive you. We all like to believe that all our characteristics are positively received by others, yet we need to be aware that others may perceive us differently. Hence, we need to be aware that all strengths can have limitations and furthermore, when we are having a bad day, we may behave in a more extreme or exaggerated version of our natural colour! As the saying goes, stress makes us stupid....

UTILIZING DISC

As DISC is a model based on observable behaviours, we can learn how to spot the colour of someone else by focusing on their behaviour, what we see and what we hear. Once we recognize the communication style of others, not only can we value their differences, we can adapt our individual style, showing more versatility, for more effective communication, influence and relationship building.

The best way to determine the style of someone else is to consider one axis at a time - which side of the mid-point are the behaviours you **observe**? This is all about big broad brush stokes so it does not matter how far along the axis they are so long as you can decide introvert or extrovert, logical / task-oriented or emotional / people oriented. Considering the style the person is least like is often the easiest start point and will immediately tell some behaviours that must be avoided. Also, seek clusters of clues rather than just one and beware of behaviours that are job-related, rather than style related. Just because someone is in finance and good with numbers does not mean they are blue. There are tendencies for people to choose roles linked to strengths and motives, yet they are not exclusive. In the same way, no one colour is associated with leadership!

Such observational skills are not limited to face-to-face settings. With practice, it is possible to listen for clues over the phone or on video sessions to determine someone else's style. For example, clues associated with introversion or extroversion can be determined by speed of speaking, volume etc. Clues associated with task or people orientation come from what they say, for example the level of formality, directness and content that is more focused on facts or people topics. In summary, the x axis clues are from body language; Y axis clues are heard in speech and what people say.

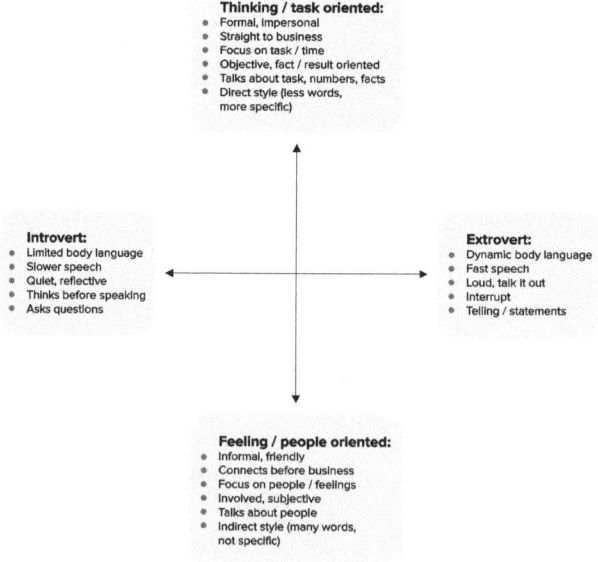

Figure 39: The clues for observing and identifying the DISC style of others

Once you have learnt to observe others, the next step is choosing to adapt your own communication style to be more impactful. In other words, communicating to others how they like to hear things, not necessarily how you would naturally do it. The question to ask is: How can I change little things about my behaviour that will avoid tension or, more significantly, enhance my influence when I deal with this person? The key is simply being versatile. By taking time to see what we can do differently and do better, we are more likely to present ideas or be more successful in achieving buy-in from others. To do this, consider the verbal and non-verbal elements to adapt.

To reds, be more specific, to the point, focus on results. In other words, give them the executive summary. Also be seen to speak up and speak quickly.

To yellows, it is more about exploring ideas and options, but also be prepared to make small talk before business and then enter friendly dialogue. Smiles are important as well as an open and more optimistic consideration of ideas and concepts. And ask a yellow for their opinion.

To greens, never push. They need softer, calmer atmospheres and need to be listened to. This means considering non-verbal communication to avoid dominating a green person. Speak slowly, ask questions, give time for reflection. Actively ask for their input, yet do not force decisions. If necessary, give space and come back later.

To blues, be straight to facts and allow them time to analyze data. Recognize their expertise, never push opinion over fact and keep discussions professional. They will ask for and need the details. For example, if you are a yellow influencer and are talking to a blue person, you must remember that they will need many more facts and data than you. They will also prefer to communicate in a more direct and specific manner and not waste time discussing the weather!

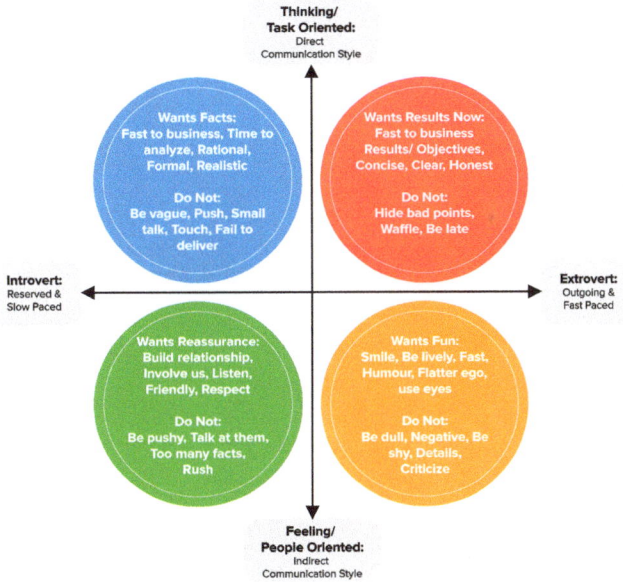

Figure 40: Summary of how to communicate to the DISC profiles

DISC is a tool. It is not the only aspect of great communication, however, using DISC however can aid influence and avoiding conflict, by valuing another person and choosing to communicate with them in the way they prefer, by simply being more versatile. DISC is a way to celebrate differences and because it is based on observable behaviours, it can be learnt!

> **Key Learning Points on Communication Skills**
> - Communication goes wrong when we don't understand the importance, skills or process, especially in virtual scenarios when we lose visual clues and distance can limit relationship building
> - Great communication seeks to build relationships and connect with others. It should be planned, starting with setting a goal, and crafted with the audience needs first
> - Audience-centric content / messages explain the why first, mix factual and emotional aspects, use familiar and simple language, and are therefore relevant and clear on what the sender expects from them
> - The modality / methods used to deliver meaning should support the message and mixed use of body language, text, images, sounds etc make messages more memorable
> - Common communication tools in business include mail, email, meetings, telephone, video conferencing, workshops, events, online forum and social media
> - To be interactive, for exchange of information in real-time, two-way genuine dialogue is essential. Exchange should not be one-directional
> - Dialogue is connecting with others. Empathetic listening and asking questions are powerful ways to engage others
> - The sender should always be willing to adapt how they communicate to individual receivers or situations
> - Effective communication is an essential ability, or competency, for personal and business success

Reflection Task	Using a rating score of 1 to 10 with 1 being "could be much better" and 10 "excellent", how would you rate yourself for each of these elements:	
Communication skills	Behavioural anchors	Rating (1-10)
Expressing ideas, facts and information consistently and inspirationally, in an audience-appropriate manner	<ul><li>Communication planning</li><li>Defining outcomes</li><li>Considering perspectives</li><li>Choosing simple language to avoid misinterpretations</li><li>Adding emotional connectors</li><li>Mixing modalities</li></ul>	
Empathetic listening to show care and respect	<ul><li>Giving full attention</li><li>Considering body language</li><li>Maintaining neutrality</li><li>Listening to understand, not interrupt</li><li>Allowing silence</li><li>Following up</li></ul>	
Using questions to engage others	<ul><li>Utilizing questions more than statements</li><li>Asking open questions</li><li>Promoting cooperation and problem solving through dialogue</li><li>Willing to gently probe further to increase understanding</li></ul>	
Adaptability	<ul><li>Understanding situational or individual differences</li><li>Willingness to put the needs of others first</li><li>Taking more time to build relationships and understanding, especially virtually</li><li>Showing personal versatility, not simply "my way"</li></ul>	
Does your rating suggest areas you need to work on, and if so, what will you do to improve?		
Have you received any feedback that would support or contradict your personal ratings? Why may perceptions differ sometimes?		
How do you believe you would rate for a more senior position? Would this impact your career planning?		

Chapter 8:

YOUR MINDSET COUNTS

Key knowledge

- Mindset and attitude are your thinking and subsequent actions towards others
- Settled thinking and habitual responses can lead to too quick judgements on people and situations which stifle others and limit openness to new ideas or perspectives
- Attitude is the most difficult characteristic to change or develop

 Key models

- Trust, not control
- Life-long learning and growth, not fixed thinking
- Challenging personal assumptions and bias
- Valuing differences
- Adaptive decision making to include others

 Impact

- An openness for inclusiveness and compassion increases the likelihood for success with others as people reciprocate in kind, are more willing to engage and go the extra mile

Mindset is all about the assumptions, methods, or notions we hold. In other words, our attitude. As a rule, attitude is a settled way of feeling or thinking about something or someone. It is therefore obvious that leaders need a more open mindset than most to be able to connect with people, achieve success with people, be inclusive of all people and ideas, even show compassion.

> *If you do not intentionally include, you unintentionally exclude.*
>
> Neil Lenane (133)

Success in the business world is not only revenue, profit or market share. Success in great companies is about the commitment to the organization, the contributions made by all employees and fulfilment of personal and business goals. Leaders achieve this by balancing their focus on the tasks, as well as on people. When seen too focused only on tasks, the impression made is like Rambo – too much demanding and pressure to deliver results. It may be easier, and faster, to tell people what to do yet it is not engaging or motivating. As the African proverb wisely notes, "If you want to go quickly, go alone. If you want to go far, go together." On the flip side, if it's all about cake on Fridays and no concern for deadlines, you may well be liked but no one succeeds. Understanding that achievement of results only happens when people buy-in, indicates the need to care about people. This means building trust, all fostered through great communication, positive influence and creating a safe environment in which everyone can thrive. If you want to learn more on how transformational leadership really builds such business success, we recommend our book, "Connectedness: Leadership for a Changing World" (42).

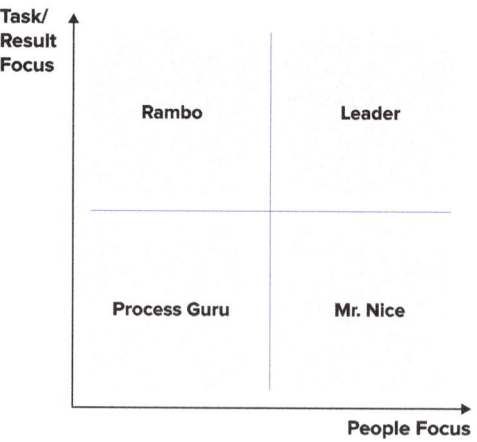

Figure 41: Leaders achieve success by balancing result and people focus (42)

HOW YOU THINK CREATES AN ENVIRONMENT OF TRUST OR CONTROL

We have talked a lot about trust, as the precursor for employee engagement and organizational commitment, and as the foundation for connecting with people and building relationships. In the world of leadership, trust is also the core of cutting-edge thinking. Where management is focused on control, highly effective leadership is focused on trust. One such trust-based model is the Extended Transformational Leadership Model (42) which is proven to be a winning approach in highly complex and rapidly changing environments. It is also more effective with virtual workers and remote teams.

In terms of mindset, trust is an abstract attitude of dependability and a feeling of confidence and security that the other person also cares (134). Trust is also a complex neural process. Mistrusting someone is not just a belief or fear of betrayal, but a negative emotional feeling about the untrustworthiness of a person. It also has to be understood that trust is rarely absolute and is restricted to specific situations. In this context this might help to explain why trust may be easier to establish when based on professional credibility, expertise and proven performance.

As a leader, the willingness to trust begins with a willingness to share; to share information on the business, as well as personal information and this trust is linked to self-esteem (135). Though the connection is complex, both trust and self-esteem are vital to social functioning. Trustworthy leaders are genuine people willing to demonstrate their values and commitment to others through their work and actions. Such leaders do not exercise their authority or hold themselves to a different standard than they hold their people. They do not control others; they create a safe work environment where all individuals are appreciated. This is important because what leaders think about people influences the their our behaviour and that of the team (136).

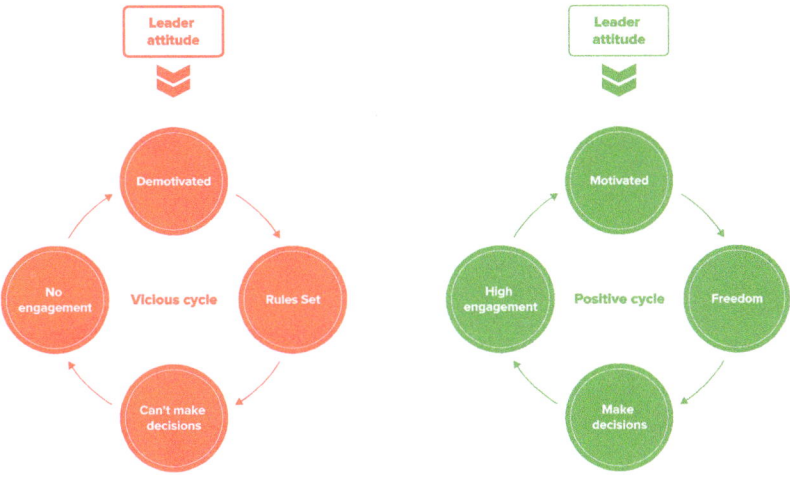

Figure 42: The power of attitude (136)

Looking at figure 42, it can be seen how the attitude of the leader makes a difference. Starting with a control mindset drives a vicious cycle (136). For example, if you believe people are demotivated or untrustworthy, you would set rules which would limit their decision making, which would reduce their engagement and hence prove your point! With an attitude of trust, the exact opposite happens. Your attitude and your behaviour really impact others, furthermore, trust and control really are mutually exclusive.

GROWTH VERSUS FIXED MINDS

Another key aspect of mindset relates to learning. A **growth mindset (50)** describes where people see their abilities as learned traits which can be developed. Such people are open to challenges and new experiences and see failure as an opportunity to learn. On the other hand, people with a fixed mindset see intelligence and personality as static features. For them, success is about proving talent or smartness and failure means that you just don't have what it takes. Such people tend to avoid new situations and take constructive feedback personally. People with a fixed mindset are much less receptive to coaching for instance than those with a growth mindset.

How to apply such an open mindset can be seen in the differences between how leaders coach their teams to grow, and how a more directive manager would handle situations.

Coaching mind set	VERSUS	Manager's perspective
Helps team members develop own solution		Creates quick solution directly
Listens to issuess, listens to understand		Tells team how to manage issues
Asks the team to create a solution and present it		Tells team what to do directly
Queries team members about their role in disagreements		Mediates staff differences directly
Leads from behind - asks questions before creating solutions. Seeks to empower		Steps ahead / out front to create all solutions and strategies
Thinks collaboratively - invites in the views of others, combines the efforts of the team		Just gets it done to meet timelines - collaborations can wait

Figure 43: An example of a coaching mindset to develop others (42)

OUR MENTAL SHORTCUTS

At any given moment we are flooded with information, yet we can only consciously process about 40 items. Cognitive filters and heuristics allow our minds to unconsciously prioritize, generalize, and dismiss large volumes of input. These shortcuts can be useful when making decisions with limited information, focus, or time, but can sometimes lead us astray. We need to be wary of assumptions and biases.

> *The eye sees only what the mind is prepared to comprehend.*
>
> Robertson Davies (136)

Assumptions or notions arise out of our experiences, culture or philosophy of life. The assumption of "my way" is best is never true. When individuals think about problems or reaching goals, patterns are formed. These patterns are self-imposed boundaries or barriers, that keep our thinking in a framework and our behaviour, such as our communication style, is constrained in this way and not adapted to individuals or situations (13). It is difficult, yet key is never to assume, especially about what other's think or when there are problems. You need to seek to understand - ask questions, listen, consider the different perspectives of all stakeholders, discussion options and agree on the solution together.

We also need to bear in mind our susceptibility to **unconscious bias** (138) that relate to the mental "shortcuts" our brain takes based on personal experiences, as well as **stereotypes**. Formed early in childhood, stereotyping helps to cluster, yet leads to prejudice. Such unconscious biases are also automatic, shortcuts used to process information and make decisions quickly (139). Unconscious bias can prevent us from making objective decisions, overlook great ideas from others, undermine individual potential, as well as create a less than ideal work experience for colleagues through poor behaviour.

Examples include (138):

Affinity bias - When we gravitate toward people who are like ourselves, we may pay less attention to the people who are not as much like us. This can be a problem if we alienate the people who seem to be less like us and give the impression that we do not value their opinion as highly.

Anchoring bias refers to making decisions from the first piece of information that we learn from.

Confirmation bias can reinforce anchoring as once we believe something to be true, we see more evidence that supports it.

Negativity bias is when our minds react more strongly to negative experiences rather than positive ones, making us more likely to turn down opportunities or new ideas or see new people as threats and not consider the potential advantages.

Reactance bias occurs when we are forbidden to do something and then have the desire to do that exact thing in order to prove our freedom of choice.

Frequency illusion – Have you noticed that when you learn a new word you start seeing it everywhere? Our brains have a habit of trying to see patterns, so we notice things more if they are interesting to us.

CHECKING YOUR AUTOMATIC BEHAVIOURS

There are many more examples of such unconscious ways our brains work and as all brains function differently, different people lean more towards different biases. However, at the individual level, the extent to which such biases are internalized and acted on varies widely and in complex ways. If we are aware of these associations, we can bring to bear our skills and intelligence to see the risks and overcome them. Through learning and reflection, we can discover how to best decrease the pressure such biases might have our communications.

It is a challenge because in business, many actions and decisions often have to be taken fast, so our brain uses the shortcuts. However, when taking an important decision, it is essential to reconsider "important information" and slow down, be more deliberate, and more logical in our mode of thinking. This can include reconsidering reasoning, actively challenging biases, seeking new perspectives from others and reviewing all options, alternative solutions and consequences.

Thinking outside the box is another term for examining and challenging our assumptions and judgements we make every day. Having a closer look at our assumptions helps to avoid being guided by them.

Examples of incorrect assumptions:

- "She has two small kids; she won't have time to be involved in the project"
- "He is an IT person. He's probably not the best person to solve this conflict. We need someone with strong communication skills"
- "He is an introvert. I doubt, he'll be a good leader"

A leader must question these assumptions and also challenge others to think outside the box in their head. The next time you catch yourself making a judgement about a person's background or working style, stop and ask yourself if this attribute could also be an asset.

Considering assets differently also begins to challenge thinking on simplicity versus impact. **Similarity attraction** (140) risks narrowing the mind and limits success. It is natural that people get along well with people who are similar to them, share the same values, experiences and backgrounds. This makes us feel safe, comfortable, get agreement and reassurance in our own identity (141). In the business world however, we need to consider what impact this has on teams and organizations? Homogeneous teams may be easy to manage and communication simple yet can also result in no new ideas coming to the table and focus remains only on what is already known. When hiring, promoting, assigning projects and developing, great leaders actively prioritise diversity. However, a common viewpoint often quoted is "I just want the best person for the job". Diversity and ability are not mutually exclusive! Diversity is an added benefit to augment attitude, skills and experience. Though many may feel safer hiring people just like them, as they believe they know what they will get, team performance will suffer long term. The result of heterogeneous teams is success, through enhanced decision making, optimized efficiency, quality and innovation.

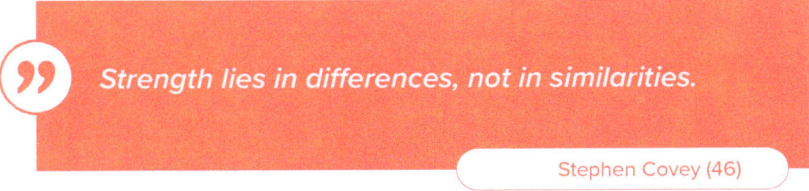

> *Strength lies in differences, not in similarities.*
>
> Stephen Covey (46)

Micro-behaviours are the tiny little things we do every day, which make another person feel appreciated, respected and included – or not. Examples of micro-behaviours:

- Looking at someone while they talk, maybe nodding in agreement – instead of looking at your phone
- Acknowledging the idea someone had – instead of showing no reaction
- Greeting someone with a handshake, saying their name and establishing eye contact – instead of saying "hello" without looking at the person

Observe your own micro-behaviours. Which ones do you use when talking to a person you feel comfortable with? Which of these could you also use with a person, you normally don't feel connected with? Remember, feeling genuinely appreciated lifts people up, makes people feel safe, which frees them up to do their best work. Feeling valued also helps avoid conflict. Conflict may stem from many reasons such as not being listened to, being overlooked or not consulted, yet the core impact is the same – people not feeling important. Treating someone in a way that is unique to them is a powerful way to make them person feel important and appreciated (2).

DIFFERENT PERSPECTIVES ARE THE SPICE OF LIFE

In terms of success with others, it is always important to remember that we all see the world from our place — never assume that other people see things the same way or value the same things as you do. Never judge others on personal outlooks. Perspective, the way we see something, has many and varied influencers (142). These can include, but are not limited or defined by, age, personality, motives, gender, background, culture, beliefs, even how you are feeling today...

And even with high emotional intelligence and well-developed communication skills, there are times when you will still get it wrong. Have you jumped to assumptions, had unclear intentions, set unreal expectations or even allowed previous upsets cloud your reaction, leading to an escalation of issues, disagreement or conflict? Then it's time to reflect on your personal actions and continue with **rational thinking** (142): In what way is my behaviour contributing to the problem? Is this issue or argument important on a scale of 1-10? Will it be important in 6 months? Is my response appropriate and effective? What can I learn from this? And if you are still down in the dumps, know your emotion shifters. What are the things that can change your feelings in a snap? Is it going for a walk or looking at a photograph of someone special? Turn to them when you find yourself angry or frustrated to shift your focus and shift your feelings. Understand your personal values and motives and understand that your feelings and your thoughts create your life - good feelings make you feel good and bad feelings make you feel bad. When you are feeling sad, bad or mad, you will never be in the best place to act!

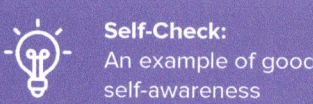

Self-Check:
An example of good self-awareness

"It's when I recognize that I am having a bad day and decide to take extra time to answer others more appropriately…"

ADAPTIVE DECISION MAKING

How we use our higher brain, our cognitive ability, involves how we reason, plan, solve problems, make decisions, think abstractly, comprehend complex ideas, learn quickly and learn from experience. This is demonstrated when given work tasks and impacts how successfully we deliver results. It impacts other people through the implications of our decisions. We also have natural tendencies for how we like to make decisions and, similar to tendencies towards a natural communication style, though we have a dominate approach, we can, and need to show **versatility** in different settings. It is important in business to be situationally adaptive and appropriate, so knowing when to make a quick decision versus when to be more analytical, consider alternatives and consequences for instance. Also, when reflecting on communicating with others, we must respect that others may have a different decision-making style. Some people have a willingness to make decisions with low volumes of information as they are more fast-acting and focused on getting things done. Others require high information volume as they are more analytical and focused on thinking things through (64). Be aware of too much information though as this can lead to poor decision quality! Beyond a certain point, our brains default to only finding more evidence to reinforce what we already know (selective search). We also risk viewing the last piece of information as the most important, simply because it is more present in the brain, known as the primacy effect. These are other bias, yet we should not get too worried about them. Our decisions are almost always based on incomplete information (143) and our brain simply interprets inputs and approximates consequences, a bit like predicting the future.

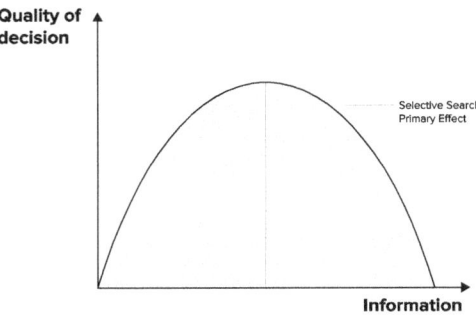

Figure 44: The decision-making paradox (42)

There are two important learnings here though. Firstly, in teams how do you work to make group decisions? Again, are you inclusive, seeking the opinions and insights of others? Do you integrate these new ideas into options and creative solutions? Do you move on discussions and commit to decisions with others?

Secondly, do you consider the quality, volume and detail level of information you share? This is relevant for individuals and a relevant factor in effective audience-centric content / message creation.

For both these aspects, don't just do what you always do, or you prefer to do. Consider the needs of others and adapt situationally and individually. And how do you know what others need? Ask them!

- What is important to you in this matter?
- Please share your opinions… Please explain your thinking more…
- Have you encountered such a situation or experience before?
- How would you fix this?
- What input do you need from me?
- What am I missing?
- How else can I help?
- What can I provide that would make this better for you?

THE CHOICE TO CARE

Communication skills and emotional intelligence are only part of the story when it comes to truly choosing to include others and build relationships. Developing emotional intelligence develops parts of the brain that also increases ability to focus on the right things. It helps us pay attention to the important things, for example our ability to notice body language, and rapport strengthens our curiosity in others so we can learn to ask more. The choice to care about how other people feel and how you make them feel may be the most important part though. As said, it starts with empathy yet goes much further. Empathy is resonating with someone else, their pain for example, yet you don't have to like the person (12). To show care however, you need to go to the next level, to cultivate an attitude of loving kindness, or **compassion**, towards people. In this context, compassion incorporates the intention to act (12). It means communicating with the intention to connect with someone, to understand a person or situation, and to make the situation better. It is being generous and often humble; it requires time and a conscious shift from reactive responses to well thought through messages and conversations. This is because communication has impact on the **self-esteem** of others. If self-esteem is hurt, the communication quality suffers. Optimal communication increases the self-esteem of participants and only by honouring self-esteem is a real win-win achieved (37, 38).

There is also one more reason to demonstrate compassion, and that is it will make you feel better! When we respond with compassion, our brain released opiates and oxytocin, hormones which create trust and closeness (12). The human brain is set up for **interpersonal integration**, allowing us to nurture differences, maintain our unique identity and still cultivate connections with others (144). Being connected to others makes us happier and more fulfilled.

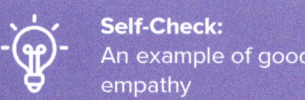

Self-Check:
An example of good empathy

"It's when I forget about getting the updates I need and focus more on what my team needs…"

Key Learning Points on Mindset
- Our mindset is our assumptions or notions we hold, how we see the world. Attitude is how we interact with the world according to how we see things
- Unlike skills, mindset and attitude can be more fixed and more difficult to shift, yet we do have control over mindset and attitude should we choose to use it
- Habits that need self-checks include negative assumptions, judgements, stereotyping and biases or shortcuts when working quickly
- New patterns of behaviour include considering others' perspectives, honouring self-esteem of others, showing generosity with time and appreciation, coaching others and focusing on results
- Trust is once again the precursor to choosing where to start
- Practicing inclusiveness and compassion will increase personal happiness and fulfilment and do not have to be limited to home or family life. They have a place in business too!

Reflection Task	Personal notes
Danger areas – which habits may you fall into? • Negative assumptions • Judgements • Stereotyping / shortcuts	
What triggers these habits or when does your brain get hijacked like this?	
What will you do to improve?	
How could you show more inclusiveness at work?	
Learning compassion requires practise so how about trying some small actions:	• Help someone you don't know • Say sorry when you interrupt people • Let someone jump the queue in front of you • Show happiness for someone when they succeed

Chapter 9:

PRESENCE OR BEING PRESENT?

Key knowledge

- Presence is physical and has a direct impact on others
- Being present is essential for team spirit and team effectiveness, and includes active participation in teamwork
- Positive presence appears welcoming to others and is linked to building rapport

 Positive behaviours

- Balanced composure for appropriateness at work
- Making a good first impression through appearance, communication and behaviour
- Actively engaging others, even when you feel uncomfortable, by asking questions, listening, good eye contact, good body language and allowing others to shine
- Sharing who you are or your own story as a positive narrative and digital image

 Impact

- Projecting and establishing professional respect through demonstrating engaging and respectful behaviours towards all others and at all times

In the workplace we need to appear to be "present", to be seen, to be there. Presence is also taken to include personal appearance or bearing, hence a leader needing to show a positive demeanour. What is generally accepted is that **presence is physical** and includes participation. It is a personal ability and active mechanism for making one's character known to others, including expressing opinions and exerting influence through image, spoken word and body language.

Presence can also be linked to the emotional competence of **composure**, and one that affects others and is therefore required in balance (123, 64). Composure is described as the ability to remain cool and unflustered in the face of frustrations or difficulties. Yet if too highly composed, you will appear uninvolved, indifferent, or remote, but too low can result in overreacting emotionally and not making sound judgements.

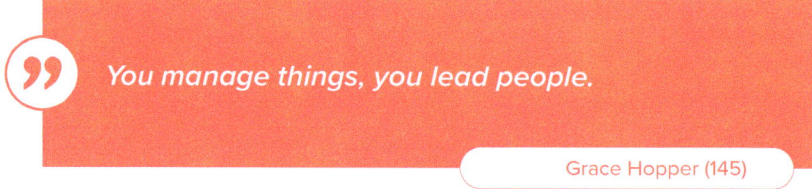

You manage things, you lead people.

Grace Hopper (145)

Being present (physically or virtually), and being available when others need to talk, need advice, need guidance or reassurance is part of good leadership. Giving generously of your **time** is part of it. However, with so much to do, focus often falls on the easier, more tangible and measurable tasks of management. Leadership on the other hand requires much more effort and generosity towards others. How much time do you think managers spend managing things, and how much time leading people? In surveys, 79% of managers say they have too little time for leadership tasks, yet only 9% say they have too little time for managerial tasks (146).

Beyond attendance, how you come across one-to-one, in group meetings and online also counts and within your control. It is vital to consider the impressions you make.

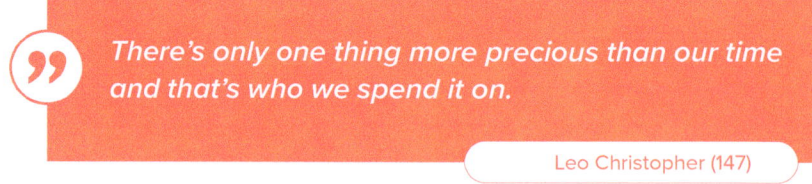

There's only one thing more precious than our time and that's who we spend it on.

Leo Christopher (147)

WHY FIRST IMPRESSIONS COUNT

In the business context, professionalism counts, as it is about demonstrating skills and competencies for doing the job well. The most highly ranked skill for professionalism is communication, with appearance ranking second (1). As the saying goes "first impressions count" and impressions individuals give to others greatly influence how they are viewed and treated at work. It is because, as humans, we are programmed to make quick judgements — it comes back to our shortcuts and bias again! Yet even when we believe we are being rational in our thinking, we can still be misled.

Attempts to observe others and their behaviour, free from any interpretation, can be hindered by observational errors. We are also prone to logical mistakes such as assuming people who speak well have deep thoughts. The halo effect is the tendency for an impression created in one area to influence opinion in another area. For example, the overall impression of a person that "she is nice!" impacts evaluations of that person's specific traits such as "she is also smart!".

Even after initial impressions have past, and we have interacted with people face-to-face, we continue to be influenced by people's **appearance** (148). Behavioural confirmation or self-fulfilling prophecy ensures we look for information which confirms our expectations. Furthermore, facial cues are extremely powerful in shaping interactions, even in the presence of other information.

What does this all mean? We need to be aware of appearance and body language!

Appearance includes digital image as already covered in chapter 5. Clothes, accessories and even footwear help to reinforce or diminish skills and qualities in the eyes of others (1). We are not going to discuss fashion here, except to say, dress smart if you wish to be taken seriously. What we do want to dig deeper into is the balance of verbal and non-verbal communication, body language, and how this is used to interact with others in a more engaging way.

THE FIRST SEVEN SECONDS RULE

In critical first meetings, making a good and memorable first impression is key, and it really does happen in the first 7 seconds (149). So, remember to:

- Smile - Facial expression says more about you than words. Make sure it's real and warm, confident and professional.
- Shake hands - The handshake (in non-pandemic times) is the universally accepted signal of professionalism, politeness and confidence. A good handshake is a fine art - a tricky balance between a tight squeeze and a limp stroke. Additionally, if there are several people in the meeting, greet them all separately.
- Introduce yourself — Never assume everyone knows who you are, so when you shake hands also say your name.

- Speak clearly - Speak in a competent and confident way making sure what you say is relevant and appropriate. Speak slowly and talk at an appropriate pitch - people take others more seriously if they have a deeper voice.
- Maintain eye contact - People are perceived as nervous or rude when they don't make eye contact. Make sure you lock eyes for 4-5 seconds at a time, then look away to avoid stressing the other person.

For women however, getting all this right is even more tricky. Research has shown that women leaders who express more "female stereotype behaviour", such as smiling, are considered less competent whereas women who express more "male stereotype behaviour", such as more aggressive behaviour, are considered less likeable (150). All the more reason to understand communication.

WHAT DOES TRULY ENGAGING BEHAVIOUR LOOK LIKE?

As we have explored, building rapport and creating genuine dialogue is the art of great communication to engage others, establish mutual trust and maintain long-term relationships. This works when people understand each other's feelings or ideas. It comes back to many skills and concepts we have reviewed:

- **Empathetic listening** (covered in chapter 2) - Paying attention to another person by emotionally identifying with them (empathy) and showing compassion to engage through powerful questioning, listening to what is said, acknowledging others and integrating or building upon their ideas or needs
- Appropriate **eye contact** - Keeping eye contact with the person you are talking to shows that you are listening and paying attention. Eye contact is linked with respect, understanding and bonding, as well as signalling emotions, thoughts and confidence. Eye contact evokes presence. The more you look at people, the more power and authority you give off (151). This needs balance however. Remember the 3rd Point Technique? In challenging conversations, too much direct eye contact increases stress levels in others and staring can indicate hostility. Overall, using eye contact well has powerful results (152):

    o Eye contact makes your words more memorable

    o Eye contact, coupled with a sudden movement, such as a hand motion or a turn of the head, makes you more memorable and more noticeable

    o Eye contact tends to make people more honest when confronted

    o Eye contact makes others more self-aware as we become more focused on ourselves and aware of our behaviour when others are looking at us

    o Eye contact creates and deepens bonds

- Matching the verbal and non-verbal – Great communication is what you say, relevant and appropriate for the audience, and how you say it, tone and body language. Remember the axiom that communication goes wrong when words and body language don't match? It is all too easy to appear disengaged simply by how we sit or how much or how little we are actually involved in discussions. Especially in group settings, as covered in chapter 4, being seen to participate and engage with others is important for presence. This means asking questions, facilitating discussions, seeking to gain insights from all group members and sharing personal experiences

- As presence is physical, always be aware of sending positive body language signals including real smiles, eye contact, leaning in or forward and active noises. The "uh, ya" show that you understand. Murmurs, nods and saying words such as "really," "interesting," as well as more direct prompts "what did you do then?" and "what was the response?" keeps conversations flowing. Be aware of when your attention drifts though as it is easy for others to spot a glazed-over look or other negative signals such as broken eye contact, turning away, checking your watch or sighing, arms crossed, leaning back or a blank face. When listening to others, continuously re-focus your attention on the speaker and try not to think about what you are going to say next or when you can leave.

- Presence is also putting others first and allowing others to talk. Sometimes that is all others need. For example, avoid letting others know how you handled a similar situation, unless they specifically ask for advice. Even if someone is launching a complaint against you, wait until they finish to defend yourself as they will feel their point has been made, they won't feel the need to repeat it, and you'll know the whole argument before responding! Don't worry about listening and thinking as we hear 4 times faster than we talk, so we can sort ideas out as they come in.

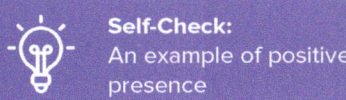

Self-Check:
An example of positive presence

"It's when I don't retaliate just to prove a point…"

But if you really want to win the hearts and minds of others, you need to make others feel important, appreciated or special:

The SPECIAL model (2):

Serve	Leadership requires generosity to meet someone else's needs or goals
Personalize	Treat people as individuals, use their name and show personal touches
Encourage	Give someone courage to start, to strive, to keep going, to stop
Courtesy	Give to all, not just those above. Never limit the please and thank you and respect
Interest	Be genuinely interested, ask, listen, respond and ask again in the future
Appreciation	Beware of complacency and indifference, share the thanks
Listen	We are captivated by great speakers but helped by great listeners so allow silence and listen to understand and show you care

CREATE YOUR OWN PERSONAL BRAND

As presence is also an expression of ourselves, a final consideration is exactly how we share our own stories. This is linked to our **personal brand**, see chapter 5, and is important because "brands" create expectations. A product or company brand and can be described as the promises the supplier is making towards a customer. Ferrari brings a promise of sports car glamour, Audi promises German engineering. Customers build trust in brands they experience or believe in and are willing to try new products just because of this trust. Personal branding is also establishing an impression in the minds of others. It is also a managed process starting from building a professional business image and delivered consistently throughout a career. It is creating a mark that identifies you and your career and one to use to express values, personality and skills (153).

Part of who we are is knowing what our story is, giving a **sense of identity** (9). Leaders need to be able to reveal an authentic side including where they come from and how this has shaped them, what they stand for, their values and their vision, and what they bring to the organization. Having the confidence to vocalize who we are may also unconsciously influence us to act in a positive way and enable us to think about ourselves in an objective way.

To create a personal narrative, firstly it needs to be positive or optimistic. **Optimism** is correlated with good mental health, decreases stress and optimists are also more likely to trust others (9). When creating your personal "one minute elevator speech", it has to be simple, starting with a captivating headline, explaining why someone should listen based on the opportunity you bring and challenges you can overcome for them and what outcome will result. In other words, using **BRIEF** (69), as we did in chapter 4, you can create a personal narrative that is focused, concise enough to overcome inattention and remain compelling enough to make an impact.

PROJECTING IN VIRTUAL SCENARIOS

As a quick reminder, the virtual world required more trust, time and technology. It also requires the same combination of characteristics for success:

- The skills and competencies for great, highly effective communication, making communication inspiring, relevant, memorable, interactive and believable, in all formats, via all tools or channels, synchronously and asynchronously
- A mindset and attitude for choosing to include others and showing compassion
- A presence that is professional, digitally visible, and available for others. It is a welcoming manner, seeking to share information digitally, building rapport despite distance and welcome inputs from everyone.

But do remember, the virtual world requires a new **digital image** and **online etiquette**. This is covered in chapter 5.

Key Learning Points on Presence

- Presence relates to our ability to send positive self-signals and use positive influence to welcome others and build rapport
- Balanced composure is required for appropriateness and leaders need to be generous in giving time to others
- Confidence and a professional appearance aid good first impressions, alongside how we introduce ourselves and welcome others
- Maintaining good impressions depends on how we seek to engage others and how we can vocalize a positive personal narrative
- Virtual presence also includes our digital image and respectful online behaviour

Reflection Task	Using a rating score of 1 to 10 with 1 being "could be much better" and 10 "excellent", how would you rate yourself for each of these elements:	
Presence elements	Behavioural anchors	Rating (1-10)
Projecting a positive self- image	<ul><li>Professional appearance</li><li>Good body language</li><li>Positive personal brand</li><li>Defined digital image</li></ul>	
Welcoming others and building rapport	<ul><li>Balanced composure</li><li>Available for employees, such as scheduled regular meetings</li><li>"Open door" for employees when they need to talk</li><li>Seeking to engage through empathetic listening and allowing others to talk</li></ul>	
Does your rating suggest areas you need to work on, and if so, what will you do to improve?		
Have you received any feedback that would support or contradict your personal ratings?		
How do you believe you would rate for a more senior position?		

Chapter 10:

MORE NEW WORLD CHALLENGES

Key knowledge

- Our complex world is ever changing
- The opportunities for personal and business growth are immense if we embrace globalization, digitalization and differences
- Leaders need to learn and adapt to the world in which business takes place

 Positive steps

- Be open to learning new skills and be willing to adapt
- Value cultural differences and show cultural awareness
- Demonstrate empathy, even compassion to all
- Be mindful of stressful situations for others
- Treat everyone as an individual

 Impact

- Leaders who keep learning, are open and care about people are better placed to improve their communication and influence, build relationships and collaborate more successfully

Our modern world of globalization, technological innovations and constant change mean businesses and leaders need to be more agile and adaptable to continue to succeed. Leadership is creating a pathway for the future by establishing direction through vision and strategies; aligning people through communication and collaboration; motivating and inspiring through purpose and trust.

For leaders in our ever-increasing virtual world, there are more changing demands due to less ability to "control" people and more need for technology use. This expands the **competencies** leaders are required to demonstrate (42):

- Leaders in the virtual or digital world need a **digital mind set**. They need to see and actively make use of the opportunities coming with it.
- **Communication skills** are also more crucial to influence rather than direct, alongside enhanced **technical and media abilities** and they are expected to foster transparency, by communicating more openly and frequently using all tools available.
- **Ability to adapt** both leadership style and behaviours, as well as communication style to engage people and connect with groups and individuals is essential.
- People orientation, genuine **care of people**, is even more important with remote workers, together with the ability to create trustful relationships.
- Leaders also need to be able to create strong **collaborative environments** across distances, including networking.
- Psychological **safety** is a critical success factor for a successful team and here, a leader needs to gain insight for each person to protect them and enable them to be in the best frame of mind for performance.
- Leaders need to show **cultural awareness**, both of their own behaviours that are influenced by own culture, as well as show sensitivity to the diverse culture of the countries or organizations where they do business.

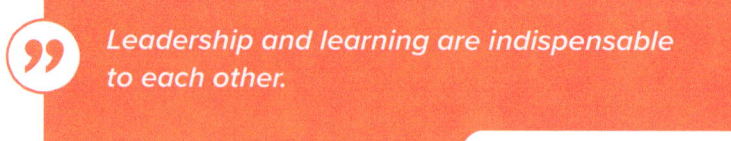

Leadership and learning are indispensable to each other.

John F. Kennedy (154)

In the global and digital world, the main aim is for all teams to feel secure. Once security and trust are established, people are more willing to speak up, contribute and gain sense of belonging, even if they are miles apart. In other words, what becomes critical is enabling teams to be better connected and to work collaboratively by creating an open atmosphere and a "sense of togetherness" and providing the necessary infrastructure and technical know-how to facilitate new ways of working success. Yes, this means spending more time working with people to ensure they and their technology work to achieve team goals. The opportunity however is connectedness that does not have to be impersonal or ineffective. Rather, great communication, face-to-face, virtual or digital, gives power to global talent and remote workers so they can contribute, collaborate, co-innovate and feel motivated by the shared experience of working together and achieving together.

	Communication Competencies	Digital Competencies	Media Competencies
Knowledge	Understanding the learnt meta-competency critical for success with others based on how we come across, our behaviours, and our impact on employee engagement	Understanding and appreciating the opportunities for digitalization for enabling virtual communication and collaboration	Understanding the impact and leveraging the power of mass communication and broader network reach
Skills	• Expressing, sharing ideas and information • Engaging others • Adapting to individuals and situations • Utilizing appropriate & mixed tools / channels • Creating genuine dialogue, facilitating discussions • Giving feedback • Addressing issues • Handling conflicts	• Using technology: finding, evaluating, sharing, communicating, storing and updating information using digital platforms • Facilitating teams to work efficiently and effectively via digital systems, tools and applications	• Analyzing and critically reviewing mass media content and form • Creating content and messages • Sharing and publishing content • Establishing virtual relationships • Building identity through self-expression
Strategies	Planning and implementation of communication that is inspiring, relevant, memorable, interactive and believable	Planning and implementation for the provision of infrastructure and tools for information flow, work processes and employee interactions	Planning and implementation of communication concepts for reach internally and externally
Mind set	Promoting and building trustful relationships	Encouraging technology integration for all	Contributing engaging information content

Figure 45: Summary of "must have" abilities for communication & collaboration today

HOW CULTURAL DIFFERENCES IMPACT UNDERSTANDING

Culture refers to the way of life, especially the general customs, beliefs and social behaviour of a particular group of people or society, transmitted through social learning. In the business world, working globally can be exciting and offer new opportunities. Many people however may be nervous about making cross-cultural faux pas and cultural differences can act as a barrier to communication, affecting ability to build connections and collaborate.

The key questions are therefore how can a leader begin to understand these differences of cultural diversity and work effectively with a team of people from different cultures and are there any further aspects of differences exaggerated in the online world?

> *Understanding other cultures builds bridges. It is the fastest way to bring the world closer together... Through understanding, people will be able to see their similarities before differences.*
>
> Suzy Kassem (155)

To be an effective globally (156), a leader firstly needs to show **cultural awareness** of their own behaviours that are influenced by their own culture. This will be perceived as different to others. Then it's about showing sensitivity to the diverse culture of the country or organization where business is occurring.

Secondly, a leader must have well developed **empathy**, able to put themselves in the position of others, as well as being open to understand differences and care about the values of others.

Thirdly, leaders must have the **ability to adapt** both their leadership style and behaviours, as well as communication style to engage people and connect with groups and individuals.

Underlying all of this is the mindset of choosing to care for individuals, taking time with individuals and building the trust needed for successful communication and collaboration.

So, what are important cultural differences that may play a part in global business? Let's look at the **Six Dimensions of Culture** model (157) and application in global or virtual teams:

Power Distance – This considers the degree of inequality that exists, and is accepted, between people with and without power. High power indicates that a society accepts an unequal hierarchy and that people understand "their place". In the workplace this may mean team members will not initiate any action, and they like to be guided and directed to complete a task by a senior manager. This could be a problem for instance with distance management, where employees are required to show more self-management.

Individualism versus Collectivism – This refers to the strength of the ties that people have to others within their community, impacting views on taking responsibility for others' actions and outcomes or one another's well-being. This could be a challenge again with remote teams spread across the world and made more difficult to overcome when only interacting in the virtual realm.

Masculinity versus Femininity – Is the distribution of roles between men and women. In masculine societies, the roles of men and women overlap less, and men are expected to behave assertively. Such beliefs could certainly cause friction in a global team.

Uncertainty Avoidance – This considers how well people can cope with anxiety and high avoidance is associated with attempts to make life as predictable and controllable as possible. This could be an issue in the virtual world where employees need competencies associated with mental agility and ambiguity tolerance.

Long- versus Short-Term Orientation - Long-term and strategic orientation tends to be pragmatic and more modest in terms of focused investment for stability. In short-term oriented countries, people tend to place more emphasis on quick gains and absolute beliefs, typically seen in religion and nationalism. Such balance is always required in business however and a manager's task in setting goals always needs to balance the short-term wins and long-term planning.

Indulgence versus Restraint – This relates to gratification of people's own drives and emotions, such as enjoying life and having fun. Here, an opportunity may arise for those desiring more social interactions to be given freedom to create online team events and build team spirit needed!

Though these dimensions may impact communication and collaboration, the challenge with such a model is that by its nature, it only describes a central tendency in society. Different organizations, teams, personalities, and environments vary widely. So, though a useful check for appropriate leadership behaviour, focusing back on people as individuals may be more fruitful.

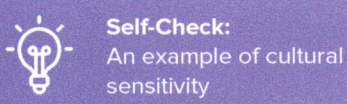

Self-Check:
An example of cultural sensitivity

"It's when I use simple words to avoid confusing my international colleagues…"

Another model, the **Lewis Model**, is rooted in concepts of monochronic or linear cultures (attending to one thing at a time) and polychronic cultures (attending to multiple things at the same time) and a concept of reactivity (158). Countries are then categorized along the 3 axes:

Linear-actives — those who plan, schedule, organize, pursue action chains, do one thing at a time. Germans and Swiss are in this group.

Multi-actives — the lively, loquacious peoples who do many things at once, planning their priorities not according to a time schedule, but according to the relative thrill or importance that each appointment brings with it. Italians, Latin Americans and Arabs are members of this group.

Reactives — those cultures that prioritize courtesy and respect, listening quietly and calmly to their interlocutors and reacting carefully to the other side's proposals. Chinese, Japanese and Finns are in this group.

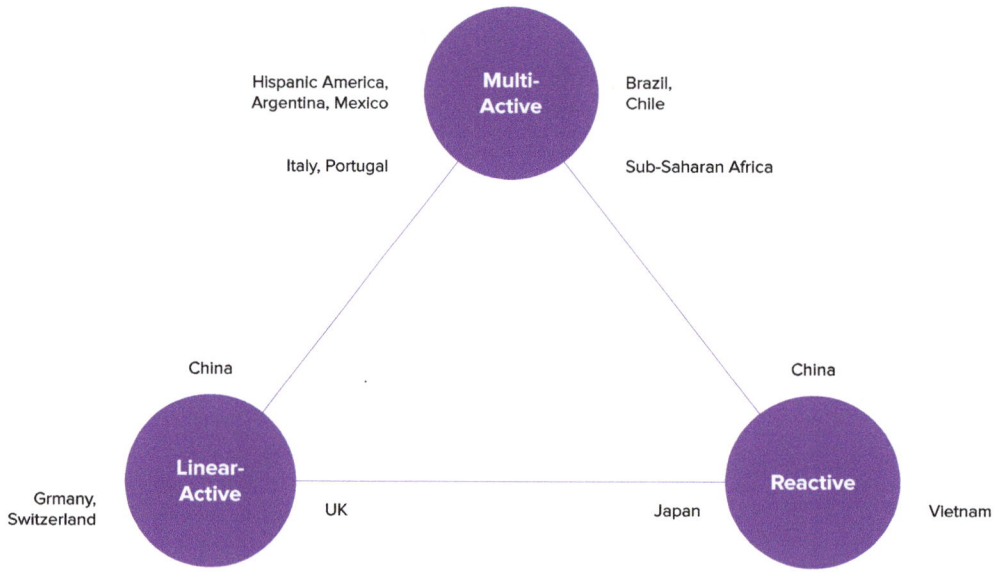

Figure 46: Representation of the Lewis Model (158)

Interestingly, during lockdown in 2020, studies took place on the reactions of teams to more online communication, such a zoom (159). What was found was the more multi-active cultures, which are warmer and more impulsive, missed face-to-face contact when immersed in the virtual world. The more linear-active groups, which they note are more transactional and factual, where happy virtually, as long as meetings where organized and controlled. Finally, reactive groups which tend to be more courteous and seek compromises are very quiet virtually.

These 3 broad category differences highlight the need for leaders to be able to adapt to different groups and different situations. Leaders need to take steps to make virtual meetings feel more like face-to-face for good energy. Establishing rules for efficiency and effectiveness and seeking to actively encourage contributions from quieter members will aid feelings of safety online. Though there is always a risk of oversimplification and stereotyping, it must be noted that this study showed that cultural groups reverted to "type" in the stressful lockdown time, meaning more exaggerated type behaviour. This mirrors personal behavioural shifts that can be observed in many stressful situations and reiterates the need for high emotional intelligence in leaders, remaining emotionally stable, with rational decision making, even under stress.

Intercultural communication is a special challenge when managing in a global and virtual business environment, yet cultural sensitivity only sets the basis for a manager to adapt, and demonstrating an individualized focus helps build genuine connections to engage and motivate others. When considering communication in the context of cultural differences, the basic rules of communication still count. Communication is not effective if people did not hear, understand or feel motivated to think differently and act differently as a result. Only when words have an impact is there success.

However, people do listen from behind their own filters, filters that may be cultural or simply individual. To inspire and engage, communication needs to be about their concerns, their issues. This means audience-centric communication, to recognize that, **when it comes to communication, it is all about the others**. The message stems from there.

> *The promotion of human values is of primary importance. We need to focus on cultivating good human relations, for, regardless of differences in nationality, religious faith, race... we are all human beings*
>
> Tenzin Gyatso (122)

Leadership is a choice, not a title or position. Developing the ability for great communication is also a choice and one that can equally be made by individual managers, project leaders or senior executives, anywhere in the world. It just takes the desire to want to make a difference.

Stepping forward to lead others, to include others in the workplace can be challenging and demanding. Once the responsibility is assumed for driving results through people, expectation also increases. Others look to leaders for direction, guidance, even reassurance. Some also judge as leaders are expected to be role-models. Understanding how you come across and how you influence others is critical. Investing time in learning how to engage others better, how to create an environment of trust and how to maintain relationships always pays off. Genuine communication inspires others, it is nurturing, and it encourages dedication to shared goals, teamwork and employee fulfilment, even happiness (160). The outcomes will be visible in terms of team spirit, productivity, business results, as well as increased respect and personal fulfilment. Other outcomes may be unexpected, such as reduced stress levels and improved personal relationships. When you begin with the intention of understanding others, absorbing yourself in genuine dialogue and seeking creative solutions with others, that is where the magic will happen!

Our challenge to you is to go beyond thinking of communication as simply informing, sharing what's new or setting tasks or projects. Broaden your topics of conversation to include sharing your dreams or vision; questioning and discussing issues and solutions with others; understanding colleagues and their needs, strengths, and ideas; showing more appreciation for differences and valuing others' contributions. Be bold - start a conversation where you do not know where the discussion will go — simply be curious and be open to learn something new.

In summary, leaders who care about people and care about their communication and influence, build relationships and collaborate more successfully. They achieve long-term employee commitment and resilience for challenging times.

BIBLIOGRAPHY AND NOTES

All of our concepts, and application over many years, are based firmly in academic studies, however, our experiences of working in global companies, have also led us to adapt and develop much of the core theories and models we have shared here. This bibliography is intended to be as accurate as possible for original sources and the thinking of other experts. We do want to make it clear though that what we have found to work, and therefore used in this book, often blends multiple concepts and we apologise sincerely if, and when, we mis-quote or modify ideas beyond their original intention. Communication and leadership are iterative, it is finding what works for you and what works in any given situation. If there was only one way, it would be easy! What we hope we have shown is that communication is something you can learn to do better every day. It simply starts with choosing to care about how you come across and how you want to impact others.

1. **Ebersole, G. (2015)**. Dress for success: The importance of your workplace attire. March 2, 2015. *https://www.readingeagle.com/business-weekly/article/dress-for-success-the-importance-of-your-workplace-attire*

2. **McGee, Paul. (2013)**. How to Succeed With People. Capstone Publishing. McGee is one of the best writers for showing how to use emotional intelligence to engage, influence and motivate people, in a fun and simple way. A highly recommended read!

3. **Clinton, William J. (1994)**. "Public Papers of the Presidents of the United States: William J. Clinton, 1993".

4. **Schulz Von Thun, Friedemann. (1981)**. The Art of Conversation. The Four Sides Model. The Schulz Von Thun Institute for Communication. *https://www.schulz-von-thun.de/die-modelle/das-kommunikationsquadrat*

5. **The HR Research Institute (2019)**. The State of Employee Engagement in 2019: Leverage leadership and culture to maximize engagement. www.hr.com.

6. **Zeffane, R.; Tipu, S.; Ryan, J. (2011)**. Communication, Commitment & Trust: Exploring the Triad. In: International Journal of Business and Management, Vol. 6, Nr. 6, June 2011.

7. **Peus, C., et al. (2009)**. Leading and Managing Organizational Change Initiatives. Management Revue, volume 20, issue 2, 2009.

8. **Capgemini Consulting (2012)**. Digitale Revolution – Ist Change management mutig genug für die Zukunft?. *http://www.de.capgemini-consulting.com/resource-file-access/resource/pdf/change_ management _studie_2012_0.pdf; 2014-09-23*

9. **Perry, Philippa. (2012)**. How To Stay Sane. MacMillan Publishers Ltd.

10. **Weforum.org (2019)**. Study Shows that Relationships Have the Biggest Effect on Health. Republished study from Knowledge@Wharton, the online research ad business analysis journal of the Wharton School of the University of Pennsylvania. 01 Oct 2019. *https://www.weforum.org/agenda/2019/10/according-doctor-biggest-contributor-health/*

11. **Goleman, Daniel. (1995)**. Emotional Intelligence: Why It Can Matter More than IQ. New York: Bantam Books.

12. **Wax, Ruby. (2018)**. How to be Human: The Manual. Penguin Random House UK.

13. **Dunbar, A. (2013)**. Solution to the 'Nine Dots' problem - thinking outside of the box. *https://www.youtube.com/watch?v=JOvjIAbB2i8*

14. **Watzlawick, Paul. (1967)**. Pragmatics of Human Communication: A Study of International Patterns, Pathologies, and Paradoxes. W. W. Norton & Company.

15. **Mehrabian, Albert. (1971)**. Silent Messages. Wadsworth Publishing Company Inc.

16. **Sinek, Simon. Author and inspirational speaker. (2020/2021)**. LinkedIn posts.

17. **Morrow Lindbergh, Anne. (1955)**. Gift from the Sea. Pantheon Books, Inc.

18. **Willingham, Daniel, T. (2006)**. Cognition: The Thinking Animal. Pearson; 3rd edition.

19. **Defalco, N. (2009)**. Influence vs. Persuasion: A Critical Distinction for Leaders. Oct. 30, 2009. Social Media Today. *https://www.socialmediatoday.com/content/influence-vs-persuasion-critical-distinction-leaders*

20. **Adams, Scott. Artist & author.**

21. **Godin, Seth. Author and business executive.**

22. **Freire, Paulo. Educator and philosopher.**

23. Five Modes of Communication are key for relating to others. They link to Martin Buber's descriptions of communication types from technical dialogue to genuine dialogue. Source: **Perry, Philippa. (2012)** How To Stay Sane. MacMillan Publishers Ltd.

24. **Huitt, W. (2009).** Empathetic listening. Educational Psychology Interactive. Valdosta, GA: Valdosta State University. http://www.edpsycinteractive.org/topics/process/listen.html.

25. **Cheng, M. (2018).** Empathetic Listening: A Six-Step Guide. https://blogs.cfainstitute.org/investor/2018/08/08/empathetic-listening-a-six-step-guide/

26. **Hohwy, Jakob. (2013).** The Predictive Mind. Oxford University Press.

27. **Shaw, George Bernard. Author (1856 – 1950).**

28. **Babcock, Linda & Laschever, Sara. (2003).** Women Don't Ask: Negotiation and the Gender Divide. Princeton University Press.

29. **Goleman, Daniel (2000).** Leadership that gets results. Harvard Business Review, 78 (2). *http://www.powerelectronics.ac.uk/documents/ leadership-that-gets-results.pdf*

30. **Goleman, Daniel (2013).** Empathy 101. 2013-10-13. http://www.danielgoleman.info/empathy-101/

31. **Hays Group Report. (2016).** Women Outperform Men in 11 of 12 Key Emotional Intelligence Competencies. Hay Group division of Korn Ferry. https://www.kornferry.com/press/new-research-shows-women-are-better-at-using-soft-skills-crucial-for-effective-leadership

32. **Drucker, Peter. Quoted in CUMMINGS, K. (2013).** Trust, Communication, and Leadership: The Three Laws of Influence. http://www.astd.org/Publications/Blogs/Management-Blog/2013/04/Trust-Communication-and-Leadership-the-Three-Laws-of-Influence (2018-02-08).

33. DISC has its origins from **Carl Gustav Jung, 1921,** where he described psychological types. In 1928, William Moulton Marston then published "The Emotions of Normal People" which describes the DISC theory used today. DISC assessments and tools are available from several commercial sources.

34. **Frost, Aja. (2019).** 48 Questions That'll Make Awkward Small Talk So Much Easier. https://www.themuse.com/advice/48-questions-thatll-make-awkward-small-talk-so-much-easier

35. **Malik, Fredmund. (2006).** Führen Leisten Leben – Wirksames Management für eine neue Zeit. Frankfurt/Main: Campus Verlag GmbH.

36. **Neuberger, Oswald. (1981).** Miteinander arbeiten, miteinander reden.

37. **Birkenbihl, Vera F. (1992).** Kommunikationstraining: Zwischenmenschliche Beziehungen erfolgreich gestalten. mvg Verlag, Augsburg.

38. **Harris, Thomas A. (1975 & 2012).** I'm Ok, You're Ok: A practical guide to Transactional Analysis. Arrow edition (5 Jan. 2012).

39. **CMI (2018).** When referring to self-awareness, Chartered Management Institute headlines claimed that "85% of people do not have this essential skill".

40. **Judge, T.A., et al. (2002).** Personality and leadership: A qualitative and quantitative review. Journal of Applied Psychology, 87.

41. **Haughton, J. (2018).** Five reasons we need to show emotion in the boardroom. 18 January 2018. *https://www.managers.org.uk/insights/news/2018/january/five-reasons-we-need-to-show-emotion-in-the-boardroom*

42. **Winkler, Katrin & Bramwell, Nicola. (2020).** Connectedness. Leadership for a Changing World. Linchpin Books.

43. **Buckingham, Marcus & Goodall, Ashley. (2019).** The Feedback Fallacy. Harvard Business Review. March-April 2019 Issue.

44. **Gunkel, L. & Mandl, H. (2013).** Acceptance and Effects of Feedback in Individual Psychological Assessments. Paper presented on the 6th International Conference of Education (ICERI), November 18 to November 20, 2013, Sevilla, Spain.

45. **Heen, S. & Stone, D. M. (2014).** Find the Coaching in Criticism. Harvard Business Review. January–February 2014 Issue.

46. **Covey, Stephen. (2004).** The 7 Habits of Highly Effective People. Simon & Schuster UK.

47. **Kouzes, J. M. & Posner, B. Z. (2012).** The Leadership Challenge: How to Make Extraordinary Things Happen in Organizations. Jossey-Bass Publishing.

48. **Schartz, Tony. (2012).** Managing People. Why Appreciation Matters So Much. January 23, 2012.

49. **Grinder, Michael. Author, coach and non-verbal communications expert.** *www.michaelgrinder.com*

50. **Dweck, Carol. (2007):** Mindset: The New Psychology of Success. New York: Ballantine Books.

51. **Proksch, S. (2016).** Conflict Management. 1st ed, 2016 [Online]. Cham: Springer International Publishing.

52. **Anonymous. (2021).** In Winkler, Katrin & Bramwell, Nicola. (2021). Trust, Time & Technology: The secrets of effective virtual communication and collaboration. *https://open.vhb.org/*

53. **Villegas, Tim. Author at Think Inclusive.**

54. **Clay, Cynthia. (2010)** in Simpson, Corey. (2010). Are you maximizing team performance, on and off the field? *https://www.comptia.org/blog/are_you_maximizing_team_performance_on_and_off_the_field.aspx*

55. **Hill, N. S. & Bartol, K. M. (2018).** Five Ways to Improve Communication in Virtual Teams. Magazine: Fall 2018 IssueFrontiersBlog June 13. https://sloanreview.mit.edu/article/five-ways-to-improve-communication-in-virtual-teams

56. **Jay, Antony. (1976).** How To Run a Meeting. Harvard Business Review. March 1976.

57. **Raasted, Claus. (2020).** Remote Meetings & Workshops. https://docs.google.com/presentation/d/1IuAii2fLeTWNxYcm1wg6Mzj80YhcfnLhg36WSTxbqgM/edit#slide=id.g7f941fdd8d_6_0

58. **Fillon, Mike. (2000).** A Handshake Is Worth a Thousand Words. https://www.webmd.com/balance/news/20000807/handshake-is-worth-thousand-words#1. Aug 7, 2000.

59. **Psychology Today (2019),** Bystander effect. From Psychologytoday.com/basics/bystander-effect. The Kitty Genovese murder case (1964) is also reviewed in the book: Bjergegaard, M. & Popa, C. (2016). How To Be A Leader. Pan Macmillan.

60. **Williams, K. D. (2007).** Ostracism. Annual Review of Psychology, 58.

61. **Dion, K. L. (2000).** Group cohesion: From "field of forces" to multidimensional construct. Group Dynamics: Theory, Research, and Practice, 4.

62. **Janis, I. (1982).** Groupthink. 2nd edition. Houghton Mifflin: Boston.

63. **Lovegrove, Harley. (2010).** Inspirational Leadership. Linchpin Books.

64. **Brousseau, K., Driver, M., Hourihan, G. & Larsson, R. (2011).** The Seasoned Executive's Decision-Making Style. Harvard Business Review, Feb. 2006, 2011.

65. **Brown, Brené. Professor and author.**

66. **Carty, Margaret. Author.**

67. **Sinek, Simon. (2009).** Start with Why: How Great Leaders Inspire Everyone to Take Action. Portfolio.

68. **Shakespeare, William. (1603).** Hamlet.

69. **McCormack, J. (2014):** Brief. Make a bigger impact by saying less. New Jersey: Wiley. Also available at, https://thebrieflab.com/

70. **Ford, Henry. Industrialist and founder of the Ford Motor Company. (1863-1947).**

71. **Alonzo, Mei & Aiken, Milam. (2004).** Flaming in electronic communication. Decision Support Systems 36 (2004).

72. **Anderson, Lynn & Anderson, Terry. (2010).** Online conferences professional development for a networked era. Charlotte, NC: Information Age Pub.

73. **Hewitt, Jim. (2013).** Facilitating Convergence in Asynchronous Conferencing Environments. *http://www.uvm.edu/~hag/naweb97/papers/hewitt.html*

74. **Inglis, A.; Ling, P. & Joosten, V. (2002).** Delivering Digitally: Managing the Transition to the New Knowledge Media (2nd ed.). Great Britain: Biddles Limited.

75. **Orton-Johnson, Kate. (2017).** The Online Student: Lurking, Chatting, Flaming and Joking. Sociological Research Online. December 11, 2017.

76. **Preece, Jenny et al. (2004).** The top five reasons for lurking: improving community experiences for everyone. Computers in Human Behavior 20 (2004).

77. **Sloffer, S. J.; Dueber, B. & Duffy, T.M. (1999).** Using Asynchronous Conferencing to Promote Critical Thinking: Two Implementations in Higher Education. Proceedings of the 32nd Annual Hawaii International Conference on Systems Sciences. 1999.

78. **Lewis, E. St. E. (1903):** Catch-Line and Argument. In: The Book-Keeper, Vol. 15, February 1903.

79. **EUROPEAN UNION (2012).** Digital Competence in Practice: An Analysis of Framework. Last retrieved 2019-03-22 from *http://jiscdesignstudio.pbworks.com/w/file/fetch/55823162/FinalCSReport_PDFPARAWEB.pdf*

80. **EUROPEAN UNION (2017).** The Digital Competence Framework for Citizens. *http://publications.jrc.ec.europa.eu/repository/bitstream/JRC106281/web-digcomp2.1pdf_(online).pdf*

81. **CREUSEN, U.; GALL, B.; HACKL, O. (2017).** Digital Leadership – Führung in Zeiten des digitalen Wandels. Wiesbaden: Springer Fachmedien Wiesbaden GmbH.

82. **INSTITUT FÜR FÜHRUNG IM DIGITALEN ZEITALTER (2016).** Führen im digitalen Zeitalter –Relevante Kompetenzen und Anforderungen an Führungskräfte. *https://www.lgad.de/web-wAssets/docs/downloads/Themenfelder-offen/Betriebsberatung-Unsere-Servicepartner/IFIDZ-Liebermeister/IFIDZ-Meta-Studie2016_Kurzfassung.pdf*

83. **Baacke, Dieter. (1997).** Medienpädagogik. Grundlagen der Medienkommunikation Band 1. Tübingen 1997.

84. **Aufenanger, Stefan. (1997).** Medienpädagogik und Medienkompetenz. Eine Bestandsaufnahme. In: Enquete-Kommission „Zukunft der Medien in Wirtschaft und Gesellschaft. Deutschlands Weg in die Informationsgesellschaft". Deutscher Bundestag (Hrsg.): Medienkompetenz im Informationszeitalter. Bonn 1997.

85. **Spanhel, Dieter. (1999).** Integrative Medienerziehung in der Hauptschule. Ein Entwicklungsprojekt auf der Grundlage responsiver Evaluation. Auszüge. München 1999.

86. **Berner, Winfried. (2015):** Methoden der Veränderung. *https://www.umsetzungsberatung.de/methoden/methoden.php.*

87. **Branson, Richard.** Founder of Virgin Group.

88. **Hendricks, Drew. (2019).** Complete History of Social Media: Then And Now. Published: May 8, 2013 Last Updated: Nov 25, 2019. In Social Media. https://smallbiztrends.com/

89. **Oberlo. (2020).** *oberlo.co.uk/blog/social-media-marketing-statistics*

90. **Bennett, Shea. (2013).** Adweek Survey: CEOs Using Social Media: Statistics, Facts And Figures. January 25, 2013.

91. **Dunay, Paul. (2014).** From Employee to Advocate: Mobilize Your Team to Share Your Brand Content. *https://www.socialmediatoday.com/content/employee-advocate-mobilize-your-team- share-your-brand-content.*

92. **Jennae, Michele.** Author of The Connectworker.

93. **Flecker, J.; Riesesecker-Caba, T. & Schönauer, A. (2016).** Sozialbericht 2015-2016: Arbeit 4.0 - Auswirkungen technologischer Veränderungen auf die Arbeitswelt. Wien: Bundesministerium für Arbeit, Soziales, Gesundheit und Konsumentenschutz.

94. **Jarrett, C. (2015).** How Facebook is Changing Our Social Lives. World Economic Forum, Octover 2015. *https://www.weforum.org/agenda/2015/10/how-facebook-is-changing-our-social-lives/*

95. **Ward, S. (2019).** What Is Business Networking & What Are the Benefits? How to Make the Most of the Benefits of Business Networking. February 04, 2019. *https://www.thebalancesmb.com/what-is-business-networking-and-what-are-the-benefits-2947183*

96. **Littlejohn, Allison; Milligan, Colin & Margaryan, Anoush. (2011).** Collective learning in the workplace: important knowledge sharing behaviours. International Journal of Advanced Corporate Learning, 4(4).

97. **Ibarra, H. & Hunter, M. L. (2007).** How Leaders Create and Use Networks. Harvard Business Review, January 2007. *https://hbr.org/2007/01/how-leaders-create-and-use-networks*

98. **de Janasz, S. C. & Forret, M. L. (2008).** Learning The Art of Networking: A Critical Skill for Enhancing Social Capital and Career Success. Journal of Management Education. [Online] 32 (5).

99. **Granovetter, M. (1976).** Network sampling: Some first steps. American journal of sociology, 81(6).

100. **Brown, E. (2011).** Strong and weak Ties: Why Your Weak Ties Matter. SocialMediaToday. Accessed on: 16.07.2020. *https://www.socialmediatoday.com/content/strong-and-weak-ties-why-your-weak-ties-matter*

101. **Clark, D. (2016).** Start Networking with People Outside Your Industry. HBR. Accessed on: 16.07.2020. *https://hbr.org/2016/10/start-networking-with-people-outside-your-industry.*

102. **Borkenau, P. & Ostendorf, F. (2008).** NEO Fünf Faktoren Inventar nach Costa und McCrae. Manual (NEO Five Factor Inventory of Costa and McCrae. Manual), Hogrefe, Göttingen.

103. **Furnham, A. & Marks, J. (2013).** Tolerance of ambiguity: A review of the recent literature. Psychology, 4(09).

104. **Raasted, Claus. (2020).** Interview. THE COLLEGE OF EXTRAORDINARY EXPERIENCES. *https://extraordinary.college/*

105. **Matt Mullenweg. Social Media Entrepreneur.**

106. **Center For Creative Leadership.** The 70-20-10 Rule for Leadership Development. *https://www.ccl.org/articles/leading-effectively-articles/70-20-10-rule/*

107. **Hough, C.; Green, K.: Plumlee, G. (2015).** Impact of ethics environment and organizational trust on employee engagement. Journal of Legal, Ethical and Regulatory Issues. January 2015.

108. **Kim, Woocheol et al. (2017).** The Relationship Between Work Engagement and Organizational Commitment: Proposing Research Agendas Through a Review of Empirical Literature. Human Resource Development Review. Volume: 16 issue: 4, December 1, 2017.

109. **Mahajan, Ashish; Bishop, James W.; Scott, Dow. (2012).** Does Trust in Top Management Mediate Top Management Communication, Employee Involvement and Organizational Commitment Relationships? Journal of Managerial Issues. Vol. 24, No. 2, 2012.

110. **Rousseau, D. M., et al. (1998):** Not so different after all: A cross-discipline view of trust. In: Academy of Management Review, 23, 1998.

111. **Hemingway, Ernest. Author. (1899-1961).**

112. **Rawolle, M. & Kehr, H. (2012).** Lust auf Zukunft - Die motivierende Kraft von Unternehmensvisionen verstehen und nutzen. Organisationsentwicklung 04/12.

113. **Kennedy, John F. (1960).** From JFK speech in Raleigh, North Carolina, September 17, 1960. *https://www.jfklibrary.org/archives/other-resources/john-f-kennedy-speeches/raleigh-nc-19600917.*

114. **Kühl, S. & Matthiesen, K. (2012).** Wenn man mit Hierarchie nicht weiterkommt: Zur Weiterentwicklung des Konzepts des Lateralen Führens. In: Die Zukunft der Führung. Grote S (Ed); Heidelberg: Springer Gabler.

115. **French, J. R. P., JR., & Raven, B. (1959).** The bases of social power. In D. Cartwright (Ed.), Studies in social power. University Michigan.

116. **Harvard Mental Health Publishing. (2011)** In Praise of Gratitude. Harvard Mental Health Letter, Nov 2011.
https://www.health.harvard.edu/newsletter_article/in-praise-of-gratitude

117. **Eisenberger, Naomi. (2012).** The Neural Bases of Social Pain: Evidence for Shared Representations with Physical Pain. Psychosomatic Medicine, 74.

118. **Kahn, William A. (1990).** Psychological Conditions of Personal Engagement and Disengagement at Work. Academy of Management Journal. 33 (4).

119. **Edmondson, Amy. (1999).** Psychological Safety and Learning Behaviour in Work Teams. Administrative Science Quarterly, 44.

120. **Duhigg, Charles. (2016).** What Google Learned From Its Quest to Build the Perfect Team. New Your Times, February 25, 2016.

121. **Radecki, Dan et al. (2018).** Psychological Safety; The key to happy, high-performing people and teams. Academy of Brain-based Leadership.

122. **Gyatso, Tenzin. 14th Dalai Lama.**

123. **Brousseau, K. & Driver, M. (2004).** Career View: Roadmaps for Career Success. Decision Dynamics LLC.

124. **Orem, T. R., et al. (2019).** Amygdala and prefrontal cortex activity varies with individual differences in the emotional response to psychosocial stress. Behavioral Neuroscience, 133(2).

125. **Erpenbeck, J. & Von Rosenstiel, L. (2003).** Handbuch Kompetenzmessung. Stuttgart: Schäffer-Poeschel.

126. **Tubbs, S. L., & Schulz, E. (2006).** Exploring a Taxonomy of Global Leadership Competencies and Meta-Competencies. Journal of American Academy of Business, Cambridge, 8(2).

127. **Shannon, C. E., & Weaver, W. (1948).** The Mathematical Theory of Communication. Urbana, IL: The University of Illinois Press.

128. **Linley, Alex. (2008)** Average to A+: Realising strengths in yourself and others. Coventry, UK: CAPP Press (2008), 9.

129. **Gruenfeld, D. (2013).** Power & Influence. Mar 13, 2013. *https://www.youtube.com/watch?v=KdQHAeAnHmw*

130. **Huang, L. et al. (2011).** Powerful postures versus powerful roles: which is the proximate correlate of thought and behavior? Psychological Science. January 2011, Vol. 22, Issue 1.

131. **Mühleisen, S. & Wagner, E. (2005)** Fünf Faktoren für den erfolgreichen Wandel. In: Personalmagazin, 7/2005.

132. **Crawford, C.B. & Strohkirch, C.S. (2006).** The Critical Role of Communication In Knowledge Organizations: Communication Apprehension As A Predictor Of Knowledge Management Functions. Journal of Knowledge Management Practice, Vol. 7, No. 4, December 2006.

133. **Lenane, Neil. Business Leader of Talent Management**

134. **Thagard, Paul. (2019).** Treatise on Mind and Society. Oxford University Press.

135. **Weining, Ashlee N. & Smith, Elizabeth L. (2012).** Self-Esteem and Trust: Correlation Between Self-Esteem and Willingness to Trust in Undergraduate Students. Inquiries Journal. 2012, VOL. 4 NO. 08.

136. **McGregor, Douglas M. (1960).** The Human Side of Enterprise. New York, McGraw-Hill Book Company, Inc.,

137. **Davies, Robertson. Author.**

138. **How Much Can You Trust Your Brain? (2018).** How It Works, Issue 118.

139. **Hunt, V.; Layton, D.; Prince, S. (2015).** Diversity Matters. McKinsey & Company. *https://www.mckinsey.com/~/media/mckinsey/business%20functions/organization/our%20insights/ why%20diversity%20matters/diversity%20matters.ashx.*

140. **Reis, H.T. (2007).** Similarity-Attraction Effect. Encyclopedia of Social Psychology. DOI: *http://dx.doi.org/10.4135/9781412956253*

141. **Blanchard, K. (2011).** *https://leadingwithtrust.com/category/circles-of-trust/*

142. **McGee, Paul. (2005).** SUMO Shut Up, Move On. Capstone Publishing Ltd.

143. **Sigman, Mariano. (2017).** The Secret Life of the Mind. Little, Brown and Company.

144. **Siegel, Daniel J. & Payne Bryson, Tina. (2012).** The Whole Brain-Child. Constable & Robinson Ltd.

145. **Hopper, Grace. (1987)** "The Wit and Wisdom of Grace Hopper". The OCLC Newsletter, No. 167, March/April 1987.

146. **Hays plc. (2014). HR Report 2014/2015:** Schwerpunkt Führung. from *https://www.hays.de/personaldienstleistung-aktuell/studie/hr-report-2014-2015-schwerpunkt-fuehrung*

147. **Christopher, Leo. Author.**

148. **Zayas, V. (2016).** Impressions Based on a Portrait Predict, 1-Month Later, Impressions Following a Live Interaction. Social Psychological and Personality Science 2016 and quoted in *https://www.express.co.uk/news/uk/737712/first-impression-judgement-people-research 2016*

149. **PITTS, A. (2013).** You Only Have 7 Seconds To Make A Strong First Impression. Apr. 8, 2013. *https://www.businessinsider.com/only-7-seconds-to-make-first-impression-2013-4?r=US&IR=T*

150. **Catalyst (2007).** The Double-Bind Dilemma for Women in Leadership. Damned if you do, Doomed if you don't. https://www.catalyst.org/research/the-double-bind-dilemma-for-women-in-leadership-damned-if-you-do-doomed-if-you-dont/

151. **Glass, Lillian. (2012).** The Body Language Advantage. Fair Winds Press.

152. **Harbinger, A.J. (2015).** 7 things everyone should know about the power of eye contact. Art of Charm. Source: *https://www.businessinsider.com/the-power-of-eye-contact-2015-5?r=US&IR=T*

153. **Peters, Tom. (1997).** The Brand Called You. August 31, 1997. Fast Company Magazine.

154. **Kennedy, John F. (1917 - 1963).** Speech prepared for delivery in Dallas, November 22, 1963.

155. **Kassem, Suzy. (2011).** Rise Up and Salute the Sun: The Writings of Suzy Kassem. Awakened Press.

156. **Koch, E. (2008).** Entwicklung interkultureller Managementkompetenz: Das Vier-Stufen-Prozessmodell. In: Koch, E. & Speiser, S. (Hrsg.) Interkulturelles Management. München: Rainer Hampp Verlag

157. **Hofstede. G. (2001).** Culture's Consequences: Comparing Values, Behaviors, Institutions and Organizations Across Nations", Second Edition. Thousand Oaks, California: SAGE Publications.

158. **Lubin, Gus. (2013).** The Lewis Model Explains Every Culture In The World. Business Insider. Sep 6, 2013.

159. **Addison, Martin. (2020).** Remote management and cross cultural communication. A Webinar for L&D Professionals. 7 May, 2020. *www.videoarts.com*

160. **Bellet, Clement.; De Neve, Jan-Emmanuel.; Ward, George. (2019).** Does Employee Happiness have an Impact on Productivity? (October 14, 2019). Saïd Business School WP 2019-13.

ACKNOWLEDGEMENTS

Our passion for great communication and leadership stems from having had the privilege of working with many great leaders and the privilege of being part of their journeys of self-discovery and learning to be great communicators. Such progress can be hard; it's life. The rewards though, for the individuals, their colleagues and for us have been immense. We are honoured to work with those who strive hard every day to make a difference. Thank you to all of you as you have inspired us to write this book.

We want to specially thank Lothar Fuhr, our training colleague and dear friend. It was Lothar who always reminded us and workshop participants "it is better to be kind than to be right". May we all live each day with curiosity, courage and kindness.

A huge thank you goes to Paul McGee, aka the SUMO guy, not only for his inspiration on great communication, but also his personal encouragement and generosity. Paul you really are a role model!

To our champions Kari Krogstad, Thomas Dobmeyer, Harley Lovegrove and Line Raquet, a big thank you for believing in our approach to leadership and communication and sharing your practical examples from your own implementation. Your willingness to challenge us and your abilities to make sense of complexity, provide new perspectives and guide positive outcomes have ensured that we keep learning and growing, both personally and professionally.

To our proof-readers Emma Caldwell and Rose Grayson, we extend a massive thank you for your time and diligence to review our message, our flow and our spelling! It is your inputs that enable us to share our concepts in a way that others can also enjoy them more. Many others have also generously shared their time, including Sophie Grayson and Anatol Ursu. We are extremely grateful for all their support.

INDEX OF KEY TERMS

2-way reach ... 73, 76
3rd point technique ... 43-44, 146
4-sides model ... 36-39
5-aspects of great communication ... 61, 98, 161
6-dimensions of culture ... 156-157
7-points to conflict resolution ... 46
70/20/10 learning concept ... 96

ABC model ... 44-45
Adaptable communication ... 32-35, 62, 123-128, 154-155
Adaptable decision making ... 138-139
Adult learning ... 94-95
AIDA model ... 78
Appreciation ... 22, 36, 41, 42-42, 102, 115, 148, 161
Assumptions ... 15, 21, 22, 24, 26, 42, 53, 110, 135-136, 138
Asynchronous ... 52, 61, 70, 74-75, 80, 120
Attitude ... 28, 46, 87, 131-134, 140
Authenticity ... 23, 83, 97, 108-110, 115, 123, 148
Availability ... 52, 71, 144, 149
Axioms ... 15, 47, 98, 100

Balance ... 37, 60, 108, 115-117, 144-146
Balanced engagement ... 60
Bias ... 56, 103, 135-136, 139, 145
Blind spots ... 16, 41
Body language ... 54-55, 62, 110, 115, 118-120, 126, 140, 144-147
BRIEF model ... 65-68, 78, 148
Bystander apathy ... 56

Care ... 22-28, 61, 69, 107-110, 114, 122, 132, 140, 148, 154, 156, 161
Characteristics model ... 48, 71, 88, 107
Coaching ... 41-42, 45, 134
Coaching mindset ... 134

Cohesive groups ... 55-57
Collaboration ... 28, 46, 52-53, 58-59, 68-71, 75, 79, 83, 105, 154-157
Collaborative dialogue ... 46
Connecting ... 22-25, 47, 69, 83-86, 98, 110, 117, 122, 133
Conscious group styles ... 58-59
Content creation ... 78, 117-118
Commitment ... 28, 39-40, 46, 96-103, 122-123, 161
Communication channels ... 70, 79-83, 120-122, 155
Communication goals ... 18-19, 36-37, 39-40, 46, 53, 54, 74, 77, 116
Communication modalities ... 115, 118-120, 122
Communication tools ... 70-71, 75-80, 120-122
Communication skills ... 14, 24-27, 94, 114-128, 155
Communication process ... 116-117
Compassion ... 23-25, 28, 61, 122, 140, 145
Competencies ... 23, 27, 47, 79, 105, 108-109, 114, 154-155, 157
Composure ... 144
Conflict management ... 15, 46-47
Conversation phases ... 39-40
Courage ... 23, 35, 95, 107, 148
Culture ... 69, 125, 138, 154, 156-159
Curiosity ... 85, 107, 140

Dialogic communication ... 120-121
Dialogue ... 22-28, 32, 40, 45-46, 58, 61, 80, 86, 98, 115, 126-127, 146, 155, 161
Digital competencies ... 47, 79, 155
Digital image ... 81, 87, 148-149
Digital mind set ... 79, 155
DISC model ... 33-35, 123-128
Discussions ... 16, 18, 22, 47, 54, 57, 60
Distance ... 19, 51, 55, 68-71, 88, 105

Engagement ... 21, 28, 55, 60, 64, 82, 96-101, 114, 155
Emotional intelligence ... 22-24, 41, 86, 107-110, 140, 159
Empathy ... 24-28, 55, 105, 109-110, 115, 140, 146, 156
Empathetic dialogue ... 23-24, 115
Empathetic listening ... 23-26, 39, 58-59, 110, 115, 146
Eye contact ... 26, 43, 118, 137, 146-147

Facilitation ... 53, 60, 99, 115, 147, 155
Feedback ... 32, 37, 39, 41-42, 45, 94-95, 105, 110, 155
First impressions ... 125, 145-146
Formal communication ... 36-39, 53, 60-61, 65-68

Generosity ... 22, 61, 144, 148
Genuine dialogue ... 22-26, 32, 40, 101, 146, 155, 161
Groupthink ... 56-57
Group dynamics ... 56-57, 77
Group phenomena ... 55-57, 70, 77
Group settings ... 52, 60, 62, 77, 1155
Growth mindset ... 45, 134

Inclusion ... 52-55, 58-59, 70-71, 87, 132, 139
Influence ... 15-16, 18-19, 52, 55-56, 60, 67-68, 71, 74, 83, 86, 96, 99-101, 108, 115, 145, 154, 161
Influence model ... 99-101
Inspiring ... 14, 18, 28, 61, 63-65, 75, 98-100, 115-117, 154-155

Judgement ... 24, 26, 55, 108-109, 136-137, 144, 145

Kindness ... 28, 107, 140
KISS model ... 14, 117

Language ... 17, 55, 60-61, 76, 98, 105, 115-119
Leadership competencies ... 79, 154
Lewis model ... 157-159

Mass communication ... 77-80, 121-122, 155
Meetings ... 18, 23, 37, 39, 53-60, 71, 80, 87-88, 99, 105, 115, 120, 145, 158
Media competencies ... 79, 81, 87, 155
Mental shortcuts ... 135-136
Mindset ... 107, 132-140, 155
Monologic communication ... 121
Motives ... 27, 32, 38, 104, 108, 126, 138

Needs ... 14, 22-23, 27, 33, 36, 40, 46-47, 67, 101, 104, 122, 139, 146, 148, 161
Networking ... 83-86
Non-verbal ... 16-18, 22-23, 105, 118, 127, 145, 147

Observing ... 23-24, 96, 110, 126-127, 137, 145
One-to-one settings ... 18-19, 24, 71, 99, 115, 120
Online etiquette ... 87-88, 149
Online networks ... 84, 86-87, 120
Online forum ... 76-77, 120

Pandemic ... 49, 145
Personal brand ... 86, 87, 148
Perspective ... 15, 18, 22, 32, 38, 40, 42, 44, 45, 54, 57, 84, 114, 135-136, 138
Power ... 100-101
Powerful questions ... 26-27
Presence ... 87-88, 100, 107, 144-149
Project plans ... 63, 75
Psychological safety ... 102-105

Questioning ... 25-27, 37, 60, 110, 146, 161

Range / depth model ... 80
Reach ...
Relationship building ... 18-19, 22-28, 47-48, 61, 126
Respect ... 23, 15, 45, 46, 55, 97, 100-102, 105, 110, 115, 138, 146, 148, 158, 161
Responsibility ... 41, 44, 56, 68-69, 94-95, 97, 100, 105, 116, 161

Safe environments ... 28, 55, 70, 96, 102-105, 132-133
Self-esteem ... 25, 40, 56, 102, 133, 140
Senior executives ... 67-68
Small talk ... 32, 33, 35-36
Situational influence model ... 18-19, 52, 74
Social media ... 79-83, 120
SPECIAL model ... 148
Stress ... 24, 57, 102-103, 108-110, 125, 146, 161
Synchronous ... 22, 52, 70, 75, 80, 120

TALK model ... 38-29, 62
Teamwork ... 26, 52-54, 114, 161
Technical dialogue ... 22
Thank you ... 42-43, 102, 148
Time ... 14, 28, 34, 35, 47, 52-54, 57, 60, 61, 68, 71, 84, 88, 94-95, 100, 105, 110, 135, 140, 144, 161
Tone of voice ... 17, 76, 118-119
Triggers ... 14, 102-104
Trust ... 22, 24, 26, 28, 40, 43, 52-55, 61, 68-71, 80, 82, 86, 88, 96-105, 132-134, 140, 146, 148-149, 154-156, 161
Trust model ... 96-98
Understanding others ... 22-28, 101, 156, 161
Unconscious bias ... 56, 135-137

Values ... 22, 26, 53, 97, 107-108, 136, 138, 148, 159, 161
Verbal elements ... 16-17, 118-119, 127
Versatility ... 32, 35, 123, 126-128, 138-139
Virtual communication ... 47-48, 53, 68-71, 76, 105, 122, 153
Virtual collaboration ... 68-71, 77, 79, 88
Virtual teams ... 47, 52, 77, 86, 122, 156
Vision ... 19, 22, 37, 53, 61, 71, 98-101, 154, 161

WHY model ... 64, 75, 98, 117-118